# UPLIFTI
## MOTIVATIONAL STORIES FROM
## EXTRAORDINARY WOMEN

# Inspirational
# Women in
# Business

## Dawn Evans and
## Tracey Smolinski

### +17 Inspirational Women

IWOW
INSPIRATIONAL WOMEN OF THE WORLD

a R⁹think Press company

First published in 2022 by
Panoma Press Ltd
www.rethinkpress.com
www.panomapress.com

Book layout by Neil Coe

**978-1-784529-69-7**

# CONTENTS

# INTRODUCTION

Inspirational Women of the World was created in the middle of the global pandemic during the summer of 2020 in order to support, advise and uplift women in a positive safe community.

Dawn Evans and Tracey Smolinski have been great friends since 2012, and when Tracey got to know Dawn better, she said to her that one day they would become business partners.

Little did they both know that the opportunity would arise when they both met up for a drink one spring evening with both of their partners. Dawn mentioned that she wanted to host a women's conference, and Tracey offered to help organise it with her, to which they both agreed.

So in June 2019 the ladies hosted their first joint event in Cardiff City Stadium; it was a huge success, with over 100 women in the room. They had great feedback and were excited to create a bigger and better conference for June 2020. However, due to Covid-19 it didn't happen. Dawn suggested to Tracey that they host it online, as Dawn was hosting mental health conferences online with her company Ajuda and Tracey was hosting her networking events with Introbiz, so it was an obvious choice in the current circumstances.

To assist with the promotion of the event, Dawn created a Facebook group and called it 'Inspirational Women of the World' (IWOW). They both had worked hard to build their own networks whilst growing their other businesses over the last 12 years, so they invited all their female connections to the group. Before long they had over 6,000 women in their community, which was quite staggering, to say the least.

As the women were being accepted into the group, they were invited to put up a post about themselves, and what was very obvious was that many of the women had amazing back stories, with many challenges that they had faced in their lifetime. However, what was clear was that a lot of them were suffering from imposter syndrome and lacking in self-confidence.

Dawn and Tracey realised that they needed to help and support these amazing women, and with their business acumen and knowledge created a membership that helped and supported them during a very tough time.

The membership was a great success and many joined on the day of the launch, and since then more women have joined this positive and uplifting community.

They then saw another opportunity. They felt that these women with their back stories needed to be heard, so they came up with another idea: to create an inspirational book to give these women a voice to tell their story, and to inspire others; but also to create bigger profiles and gain more exposure for these wonderful women. Again, the book was a huge success and became an Amazon No 1 Best Seller, which turned all the co-authors of the book into Amazon No 1 Best Sellers too.

Dawn and Tracey were absolutely delighted and have since gone on to organise business retreats, masterminds and more multi-author books for these inspirational women. They have also opened up an opportunity for any of the women to visit Necker Island with Sir Richard Branson, something both Dawn and Tracey were fortunate to experience back in 2019.

Dawn and Tracey are super excited to see what the future holds for IWOW and their passion for helping and supporting women, and making a positive difference is what they do best.

INSPIRATIONAL WOMEN OF THE WORLD

# CHAPTER 1:

## Ali Wright

---

Have you ever wondered about the path and choices you've made in life?

Well, here I am, Dr Ali J Wright, founder and owner of Needle Rock; a good and proper 'Chair Doctor'. At Needle Rock, we create functional upholstered furniture of high visual impact for the design conscious. If you want something different, look no further.

Using the words of the well-known song 'You may ask yourself, how did I get here?'

This is my story.

It all began with the death of my dad in 2008. A difficult man, and our relationship was often strained, but he *was* one of life's constants. Suddenly, he was not here anymore. It was not sudden, it was long and drawn out. Temporary relief, then guilt, then emptiness.

Funny how death makes you question everything. Am I happy? Why? What can I do to change? Life is just too short!

So, it begins…

Fed up at work; sat behind a desk, bored…

I found myself a new job, a sideways position. Result! I travelled the country detecting a rampant plant disease, issuing destructive orders and managing *Phytophthora* infection sites. I loved it, I was good at it and I was making a difference. Fondly, I was known as Dr Death!

Nothing stays the same. My boss left for pastures new; our team was absorbed internally. The good old days had gone. Then, an early morning call from my bestie; this was not normal. Our close friend was dead. No longer here. Departed this world and found alone in his flat. OMG, how did this happen? Why? He was just 52… yes, that's right, just 52 years old.

Fu*k, fu*k, fu*k… I can't process this… Really…? Are you sure? Am I really hearing this?

The call to work: "I'm sorry but I'm not well, I won't be in today…"

So, it begins again…

It's like groundhog day; OMG it is groundhog day…! Now I'm back at the start. But where to now?

I spent the next three months off work trying to find myself. I built vegetable beds out of stone in the garden, my boyfriend Gordon (now my hubby) making me a mix of compo in the mornings before heading off to his lecturing job. I needed something solid.

Daytime TV was full of programmes showing you how to make money with antiques or turning old junk into gold. The creative spark in me was ignited. I loved furniture, I loved painting, it was a no-brainer. I'd found a new purpose in life. Early experiments were very successful. I could pick up old brown furniture for little money and transform it into something quite decent. I returned to work on a three-day week, determined to create a new path.

Over the next few months, I'd built up a good stock of 'shabby chic' painted furniture and we headed to a Christmas fair at a local country house. We needed a name: *Funked Up Furniture*. In hindsight, not the best name after all; *Funked Up Chair* was easily misread! Poor Gordon, he jack-knifed the trailer in the driveway of the country house, blocking it for all concerned. But… what goes in must come out and after much toing and froing we were facing forwards again. We'd sold our goods, our pockets were full and we were victorious!

The business needed a new name: *Needle Rock* (www.needlerock. co.uk/about-us) was founded, inspired by an old photo of the Gulls Needle which stood on our local beach in 1905.

I attended as many business workshops as possible and set about building my new business. The logo was based on the Gulls Needle. Well, it was initially, until a business adviser suggested it looked like a 'giant penis'. I'd been on a couple of upholstery taster sessions by now and the name stuck; after all, Needle Rock had connotations of sewing and we lived near the sea.

We acquired a business base, an old cellar bar – a subterranean cave where we spent many hours getting ready for launch day. It was a total disaster. Hardly anyone attended, I fluffed my opening speech and I sold one piece of furniture to a friend. Gutted! I drank the wine intended for the non-existent guests.

Needle Rock limped on; I was still working three days a week to pay for it; the shop was open weekends. One Saturday morning, I noticed the furniture had bloomed because I'd had the doors open. WTF!

I acquired shop space in Carmarthen and a painted dresser sold in two days! Wowzer! Back on track? No such luck! Following on, a combination of high tide, excessive rain and being so close to the sea flooded the cellar bar. Finally, after struggling so hard to keep this space, the penny dropped: the cellar bar had to go and so did the furniture. This simply wasn't working. We moved lots of heavy furniture to shop spaces across the country, but they were still difficult to sell. Eventually, we auctioned them off.

I was seriously short of money, my inheritance, savings and redundancy burnt up in the dream of owning and running my own business. We'd just taken a huge dresser to an auction house near Shrewsbury and, being an addict for auctions, I'd somehow bought a rotary composter, now in the trailer. Even this didn't work and it cost me money to move on. Desperate to bring cash in, on the way home I had a telephone interview in a pub car park, pacing up and down to find reception. They sniffed desperation; I didn't get the job. The pub wasn't even open. Life was just sh*t!

At this point, I'm training three days a month for professional upholstery qualifications in Hereford. I'm learning a trade, but it's a slow process. With my redundancy money I built a small workshop at home. Every new skill, I put it into practice and offered services in Needle Rock that I could just about manage. In 2019, Needle Rock became accredited with the Association of Master Upholsterers. Professional reputation is a big deal for me.

I persevered, working in my 20m² upholstery workshop before my productivity dwindled. I'd lost my drive, I couldn't get myself in the workshop, displacement activities were aplenty. Bigger jobs were coming in; what was wrong with me, why couldn't I just crack on and get them out? I was trying to upholster a giant 2.3m Victorian sofa in a tiny workshop with all my upholstery tools, materials and industrial sewing machines all around me. I didn't have room to breathe in my workshop, let alone swing a cat; then the lightbulb moment: I simply didn't have the *space* to work. It wasn't me after all, it was the conditions I was trying to force myself to work in. I needed bigger premises.

After a chat in our local pub, a farmer became my knight in shining armour. In May 2019, Needle Rock moved to its new premises, an 80m² stone barn just up the road. Hallelujah! We installed electrics, we covered the concrete floor with kindly donated carpets and erected a summer house as a fabric store. It took a whole month to move everything, and once everything was in its place, the 80 m² was full. Hardly surprising my productivity had diminished. The flame of motivation returned. Business boomed and I was so proud to have survived the 'valley of death', not once, not twice, but three times! I was a success, I had survived. Then Covid hit.

I worked throughout and joined a Facebook group, Inspirational Women of the World (IWOW). This support network was a lifesaver when I was hit with overwhelm. I needed workshop assistance, but I had no money. Finally, after months of appeal, Needle Rock received a game-changing Covid grant. Fast forward to October 2021, I have four helpers, with a network of support specialists.

## So, what makes Needle Rock remarkable?

Needle Rock brings luxury materials, unique design and craftsmanship into the mix, giving antique and vintage seated furniture a beautiful new identity. Each piece is individually assessed and sympathetically restored. Where possible, we retain a bit of its history. Who knows, in 100 years' time, a traditionally restored piece may be uncovered again, with some original upholstery seeing the light of day once again. Saving pieces from landfill is a sustainable solution. At Needle Rock we work with our customers to create a vision that will fit perfectly into their living space, enabling you, the customer, to fall in love with your furniture all over again. You simply cannot buy this custom design on the high street.

Bring on the next chapter, I'm ready. Hitting 50 this year, I'm grateful to have made it this far. I have a fabulous workshop (too small), a great workforce, a strong network and two trusted business mentors. Sure, it won't be easy but I'm stronger than ever and I'm younger than I'll ever be again.

## Ali Wright

Dr Alison Jayne Wright, Ali, is the owner and founder of Needle Rock, a thriving upholstery business on the west coast of Wales. A self-confessed chair addict, Ali sees past the damage and works with a passion rescuing, restoring and reupholstering tired furniture into fabulous functional art.

Once a botanist, always a botanist. Despite having a doctorate in plant disease and working for more than a decade in plant science, Ali needed an outlet for her creative urge. Ali delights in sourcing fabrics showcasing the natural world, from tropical jungle plants to leaping leopards – what will land on the bench next?

Ali married Gordon Allison in March 2018. Fiercely individual, she kept her name and jokes she was 'Alison Allison' for one day only. They live in a sleepy Welsh village with their two Airedale Terriers, Maeve 'Bear' and Rosco 'Beanz'.

ali@needlerock.co.uk

www.needlerock.co.uk

www.facebook.com/NeedleRock

INSPIRATIONAL WOMEN OF THE WORLD

# CHAPTER 2:

## Amanda Anderson

---

### 'Thoughts Become Things'

A huge warm welcome to my chapter! I am so pleased and grateful to be a co-author amongst such inspirational women as these.

I'm wondering if the heading above may offer a little clue about my theme.

Firstly, a little bit of background. In 2020, (which was undoubtedly the strangest of years) and via an introduction from a friend (Sybil Fowler), I landed in a Facebook group called 'Inspirational Women of the World'. Instantly, I questioned my presence there and almost clicked straight back out, thinking, *Well, I certainly don't belong in here.*

'Woman'? Tick. 'Of the World'? Tick (human) – but I hardly qualify as Inspirational!

I settled on 'two out of three boxes ticked' being sufficient for me to stay put, for the moment. Looking back, this was a 'step of inspired action' (or divine intervention maybe!).

I was born in Cardiff, South Wales, and have spent my life here in this wonderful part of the UK. My husband and my son are my 'why'. (My son Rhys is also a creative and shares my love of words and music.) My family and friends mean the world to me, along with our much-loved menagerie of dogs, cats and other animals.

My earlier career included several roles: Building Society Manager and Administration Manager of our family-owned residential home, and Veterinary Practice Manager. Despite these roles all having fallen within the 'corporate' bracket, I am a creative soul, embracing anything from the performing arts to being 'Queen of the hot glue gun' and just about anything between which may be classed as 'creative'. When asked what I do for a living, I often lay claim to being 'an aspiring Blue Peter presenter'!

Aside to my focus in this chapter, I have also been in business alongside my husband for the last decade.

This has been a fabulously expansive experience and anyone who has built a business will likely share my perspective. Your business takes on the persona of 'your child'. You nurture it, invest in it, launch it, hopefully and tentatively, into the big wide world, lose sleep over it and celebrate it. It becomes integral to your soul.

As much as I loved this part of my life, I was always aware of a 'missing link'.

## The Missing Link

I was brought up by my maternal grandparents. My grandmother had a passion for words and placed high value on being considered 'well-spoken'. She was keen to pass this on to me and, as such, invested many a long hour enthusiastically reading to me and teaching me to read and write, long before my school days arrived. I loved my Enid Blyton bedtimes!

As a young child, I also remember getting wildly excited by the rhyming sound of 'cat,' 'rat' and 'mat,' often creating little simple poems of my own. As an adult, I have always loved to 'hobby' write (birthday card verses etc), again with poetry being my 'thing'.

About six years ago, I also became interested in spirituality, and specifically intrigued by the Law of Attraction.

Until that point, I had not known that I have *always* worked with the Law of Attraction – as have *you*! We *all* do… via our thoughts and feelings. 'Energy flows where focus goes'! I hadn't, however, been working with it *consciously*.

I have now also qualified as an LoA Practitioner and support others in positively focusing their mindset.

In May 2020, I enrolled on a free online training opportunity. It was a week-long challenge, the focus of which was 'manifesting' ('manifesting' simply means 'to create something' in your life). Most of the cohorts were wanting to manifest 'love' or 'money', whereas I wanted to discover my true purpose – my 'dharma'!

I spent the entire sunny May week sitting in my garden (aka 'my little piece of heaven') pondering the questions posed in the workbook and frantically pouring the contents of my soul into my specifically purchased dharma-finding journal! By the end of the week I had gained clarity:

"Use your words to support others."

There it was! These words randomly came into my head and have stayed there ever since. I knew my way forward.

As lockdown progressed, I had started to write on a more consistent basis. Rhyming verse continued to flow at a rate of knots. I knew that I would be publishing a book before the year was out.

I 'felt' this book! I 'saw' what the cover would look like. I knew the subject matter, the layout… the images to include, etc.

What I *didn't* know, however, was how on earth I was going to bring these things together to create a book. I had no knowledge of publishing and no idea about where to start. I trusted that the process would unfold accordingly, remembering that when working with the Law of Attraction, we release the need to know the 'How'.

## Trust the Process (July 2020)

The Universe didn't let me down.

Almost as if by magic, a lady by the name of Karen Brown arrived. Karen is also a member of IWOW and happens to be a coach/self-publishing expert! Suffice to say that it was no coincidence that Karen 'turned up'.

It is said that people appear in our lives for 'a reason, a season, or a lifetime'. I refer to this lady as my 'Obi-Wan' and she calls me her 'Rey Skywalker'!

By late autumn, my book had been written and with Karen's help was almost ready to go. I had sent a draft proof to a few publishers and had been thrilled to receive two publishing offers. The drawback, however, in proceeding with a publisher would be the delay in getting my book into print. I felt that this book was meant to be released in 2020, but *had* I accepted an offer, it would not have been published until the New Year.

I decided that with Karen's help I would self-publish.

I placed a lightbox on my desk, illuminated with the words 'The Perfect Gift' and 'No 1' (relating to Amazon No 1). Each time my eye caught it, I *felt* it. This was now happening!

My book was published in December 2020 and reached No 1 in the Amazon Top 100 Best Seller List in category.

The book is a collection of motivational and humorous rhyming verse, with a dollop of spirituality and Law of Attraction included. This had been my vision.

## The New Year Arrived

By this time, I had become 'hooked' and knew that writing would now be a significant focus in my life. Prior to publishing *The Perfect Gift* (and since having met Karen), I had also been publishing journals, with my *Dream Journal* reaching Amazon No 2).

I then had another spark of inspiration.

Recollecting my own childhood, and in particular the love for words that my grandmother had nurtured in me, I decided to create a fun learning resource for children, which supports their literacy development and creativity.

My brand name, 'Spark My Imagination', popped into my head.

This is what I hope my story kits will do for children. I was also excited and thrilled when Spark My Imagination was chosen as a winner of Theo Paphitis' (he of BBC *Dragons' Den* fame) #SBS (Small Business Sunday) competition on Twitter.

I am now perfectly aligned with 'Amanda Anderson Writer/ Creative' and 'offer my pen' to support others. This includes bespoke poetry: I offer a '60 Second Elevator Pitch' in rhyming verse to those who want to create a lasting impression at networking events!

I'm amazed and thrilled at the diverse uses that my poetry is seeing: unique product branding, meet the team introductions, birthday gifts, etc.

My next book is also on the way, themed on (you've guessed it) The Law of Attraction!

To bring my chapter to a close, I would like to share one of my poems from *The Perfect Gift* in the hope that my words will resonate with the person who needs to hear them, and encourage someone to follow their own calling.

## TIME TO FLY

My dear, I have to tell you

As you really need to know…

You did not come to play it small

You planted here to grow.

You aren't cut out for 'ordinary'

To never stake your claim…

To not show up as your truest self

You must make this your aim.

You know you hold the power

Let that Superwoman fly

There will never be a better time

To soar above your sky!

If I were to offer a few words of encouragement to anyone who may be wavering over a considered brave leap of faith (either in business or in life), it would be these:

1. It is never too late to become who you are meant to be.

2. Never underestimate the power of positive thought.

3. Take a step of inspired action today (such as joining a Facebook group).

Finally, I have also now released my rhyming Law of Attraction/ positivity themed card deck.

What is it called? *Thoughts Become Things* of course!

# Amanda Anderson

Amanda Anderson is a Writer/Creative and author of the Amazon No 1 Top 100 Best Seller in category, *The Perfect Gift*.

She accepts commissions for poetry, with her expertise being 'humorous rhyming verse', and is also pleased to offer her services as a general copywriter for marketing/social media campaigns.

Her story kits for children (Spark My Imagination) won the Theo Paphitis #SBS (Small Business Sunday) award on Twitter in July 2021.

Amanda is a passionate Law of Attraction advocate and practitioner. She is also the administrator of approximately 50 social media pages, which include charity/community groups.

Amanda is married with one son and lives in Cardiff with her family and numerous pets.

Combining her interest in charity fundraising with her love of singing and the performing arts, Amanda enjoys a recurring role as Mother Tree in the local Tenovus Cancer Care Charity fundraiser pantomime.

www.amandaandersonauthor.com

www.facebook.com/Amanda-Anderson-WriterCreative-114894294185374

www.linktr.ee/AAAuthor

IWOW
INSPIRATIONAL WOMEN OF THE WORLD

# CHAPTER 3:

## Anne Bleeker

---

### There's an entrepreneur in all of us

I always thought I would have a corporate career and firmly believed entrepreneurship just wasn't for me. Growing up though, I admired successful business owners and wondered how they did it. Entrepreneurship doesn't run in my veins or my family, and it wasn't until I unexpectedly became one 11 years ago that I realised there's an entrepreneur in all of us.

I worked as an in-house corporate communications director for over a decade and absolutely loved my job. My studies in hospitality management and business administration led me to travel the world, live abroad and work in the world's best hotels and multinationals, opportunities I absolutely relished. One day in my last corporate job, on the way back from a meeting marathon on a plane, I made a recommendation to the chairman of the company to outsource part of the communication function after a big transformation project. I felt strongly that this was the right strategic decision for the business at the time, even though it meant I had likely talked myself out of a job. Several months later, he took me up on my recommendation and suggested I set up my own business so they could outsource communication work to us. And there I was, dazzled yet excited, not knowing that this would be the best opportunity I would ever be given and the best decision I would ever make.

Looking back, this wasn't just a once-in-a-lifetime chance but also a complete life change. At the time, my husband and I both had demanding corporate jobs with long hours and lots of travel, but we also had a four-year-old who had just started school. We were juggling our careers and home well, but as a mum I couldn't help but feel guilty a lot of the time. I loved my job, wanted to work full time and thrived in my career, but I also longed to be there for Lauren as she grew up – a paradox that I'm sure resonates with many. Starting my own business allowed me to have my cake and eat it and enabled me to find the ultimate balance to enjoy the best of both worlds in my career and family. Becoming an entrepreneur changed my story.

Today, 11 years on in my entrepreneurial journey and now with a teenager in the house, I look back with a smile and a sense of serenity. Has it been easy? Absolutely not. Did I fail? More times than I care to remember. Have I wanted to quit and go back to a corporate job? I lost count years ago. Did entrepreneurship come naturally? Not at all, but I learn every day. And you know what, it's all part of my story – the good, the bad and the ugly. The successes, wins and lessons learned all continue to shape my narrative and, in turn, drive my strategic direction, goals and next steps.

I'm proud to run a successful business that helps companies with communication that drives results, whilst working flexibly and location independently so I can achieve my family and lifestyle goals. The first time I moved continents, I was worried I would lose customers and employees, but the opposite happened and it became our best year. Since then, I have moved countries several times and lived on three continents, and this has become my story.

## Flexibility with accountability

"Freedom is not the same as lack of accountability." – Kevin Powers

My business partner and I founded In2 Consulting in Dubai in 2010 as a boutique strategic communication agency with the help of the company we were both employed at, and they became our first client. We decided to create a business that was virtual by design – not by chance, size or otherwise – with flexibility and accountability at the core. This structure was unique in our field in the Middle East; from the way we attracted the best senior communication talent and worked together remotely, to how we created and delivered the best value to our clients to maximise their success.

Ever since, I have passionately advocated our virtual business model, long before remote and hybrid working became the new norm during the global pandemic, and strongly believe it not only benefits our people but brings significant value to the business and our clients. Our model has become an integral part of our story.

## Once upon a story – the power of storytelling

"Storytelling is an ancient 'hack' that is going to work no matter what." – Amman Assadi

As with everything in life, to get results you need a plan. When you start a company, you have the unique opportunity to create a blueprint, to shape your narrative, and tell your story to get your business heard by the people that matter most. As a PR and business communication professional, I can't begin to tell you how powerful and important storytelling is in business.

People may not remember the names of your products, the benefits of your service or the structure of your pricing model, but they will remember your unique story, which often is funny, inspirational or engaging – like why you started the business, how you solved a particular problem, or how you create value for people or the planet. Every company has a story, but you need to write it first.

I do a lot of work with entrepreneurs and startups, especially in technology, and I always see plenty of passion, drive, commitment and conviction when it comes to their products, solutions or services. What's often missing though is clarity, articulation and ownership of their story. It may take several meetings and conversations to decipher what they *really* do and why, and who they do it for.

We all have a story to tell, and so does every business, but you need to create and own it before you can tell it. Truth is, when the story is yours, it's easy to tell and it will become an integral part of your sales and marketing pitch. This, in turn, will guide your decision making, fuel your fire and drive your purpose.

## Build your business, own your story

Brand storytelling is no longer a 'nice to have' or something the marketing department does, it's a strategic business tool to get the results you're after, whether that's revenue, investment or exposure. You see, anyone can tell a story but not everyone is capable of telling a great story that will have the desired impact.

As communication consultants we're often seen as spin doctors or publicists, but the title I love most is that of storyteller. I'm fortunate to work with business owners and corporate leaders every day to help them create and tell their stories. Using a strategic communication process, we get to dive into their business and uncover what really drives them, what they stand for and what they want to achieve. We then develop narratives that tell that story to those stakeholders and audiences they're looking to reach, with the goal of creating an emotional connection between our clients and their customers, prospective clients, media, key opinion leaders, investors and employees. These are based on facts and understanding their real point of difference. Then, we develop a well-thought-out strategy that determines how and where we communicate their story. The channel selection is a storyteller's best weapon – after all, what good is a great story if no one can read it, hear about it, or relate to it?

In doing this, we focus on four key elements, all of which are essential to successful business communication: *Clarity* in your story and positioning, *Credibility* in your content and thought leadership, *Connection* with your audience and key stakeholders, and *Confidence* in your ability to get your message across.

Every business is unique and so are its communication needs. It's important to spend time, not just when you start out but on a regular basis throughout your business journey, to work on your story and sharpen your communication toolkit. Your products and solutions may change over time, as can your customers' needs and preferences. Add to this the plethora of new communication channels and social media platforms that become available, and it's clear that this requires your well-deserved attention.

We follow the Audience – Message – Channel approach. First, make sure to understand exactly who you're looking to reach, then what messages are needed to reach them, and next, assess what channels are best to deliver these messages to them. I know communication is only one item on an entrepreneur's to-do list, and although I'm biased, I promise you that it's vital to your success.

Starting my own business has been an incredibly rewarding experience, and although I may not have believed it at first, I know there's an entrepreneur in all of us. So, if you're thinking of starting out on your own or are keen to travel the world while running your business, I say as we do in Arabia: *Yalla* – go for it!

# Anne Bleeker

Anne is a strategic public relations and business communication specialist with over 20 years of international experience, specialising in communication strategy, brand storytelling, internal communication and content strategy.

Prior to co-founding boutique communication agency In2 Consulting in Dubai in 2010, Anne held senior leadership roles in corporate communications in multinational organisations in hospitality and manufacturing. Over the past decade, Anne has been helping businesses use PR and business communication as a strategic growth tool.

Creative thinking and a desire to help organisations find the right words, and get their message across to the right audiences, led to the creation of In2 Consulting and this has defined the agency's approach to business ever since.

Originally from The Netherlands, Anne married her high school sweetheart Floor after college and has lived abroad ever since. They have called Dubai home for the past 20 years; it's where their teenage daughter Lauren was born.

Anne@in2consulting.com

www.instagram.com/anne_bleeker

www.linkedin.com/in/anne-bleeker

INSPIRATIONAL WOMEN OF THE WORLD

# CHAPTER 4:

## Beccy Smart

### Self Belief Equals Success

Welcome to my story; a 30-year-old female entrepreneur who has worked hard to change her mindset from self-doubter to self-believer.

### You've come so far

Ever since I was a little girl I knew I wanted to have my own beauty salon. I knew that I would need to work incredibly hard and believe in myself to achieve anything and everything I set out to do. Academically I wasn't the brightest at school and I had extra support in primary school to ensure I didn't fall behind. When I went on to secondary school, my favourite subject was business; I studied business GCSE and A-levels. I worked hard; my focus was to achieve good grades. I had an incredibly dedicated and kind teacher, Miss Patrick, and with her encouragement I went on to achieve the fantastic grades that I'd worked so hard for.

I then enrolled in my Beauty Therapy course, which had always been my passion. I remember in my last year of training my lecturer speaking to us about furthering our education: a degree in Spa and Business Management. At this point I hadn't ever considered university. University I always thought was for extremely intelligent people... not me! However, I decided I would apply and went to visit a few different places.

Newcastle was my favourite and as soon as I had seen it I knew that was where I wanted to be.

The problem was, there was a limited number of places on the course and a high number of applications. I had put my everything into the application and interview process yet I still had a small part of me that doubted myself. Why do we do that? Why do we let that tiny bit of our brain think that we just aren't good enough? But I was good enough, I got my acceptance letter and a few months later I was packing my bag to start my new life in Newcastle as a degree student.

My first year at university didn't see me achieve the best results; I chose partying over essays and exams. I remember sitting in the office and my teacher expressing her concerns, she knew I was capable but I needed to apply myself and work hard. That gave me a reality check and I wondered why I was going to settle for an average mark when I could be achieving a lot higher.

So I started to say no to nights out and instead would get stuck into my essays. The course was hard and I felt it took me longer than others to get a good understanding of how to compose my essays. Choosing to study rather than partying then made me very unpopular with my peers and I soon began to feel isolated and quite down.

I began to wonder whether university was right for me. I was struggling academically, the majority of my friends were clubbing every night and I just started to question why I was even here. I remember knocking at my friend's flat door and as he opened it I just stood there crying at him. I felt like I was a failure and that I wasn't going to get through my course. I was so thankful to him for being there for me in that moment when I felt at my lowest.

I knew I was stronger than this and I knew I could achieve my degree if I really put my mind to it and started to focus. I would prove to everyone that even if you aren't the smartest you can still achieve a degree. I changed my mindset and started believing in myself. I earned my place on this course so I was determined I would see it through. I ended up achieving a 2.1 BA (Hons) and I then went on to achieve my postgraduate Certificate in Education, which allowed me to teach.

## Don't let them bring you down

After completing my degree, I managed to secure a job as a spa manager; although it wasn't my own business it allowed me to use the knowledge from my degree in my new role. I was excited for this opportunity and wanted to make a real success of it. However, this was not the dream job I thought it was going to be. Things started to go wrong quite quickly. I soon began to realise my employers employed me as a manager but they weren't going to allow me to manage the spa. They wanted full control and shut down any ideas I had. My confidence was knocked, I was made to feel worthless and I began to question myself. I would go home totally deflated and often worry if I could ever have my own business if I couldn't even manage this. In the end, the spa wasn't doing well and I was made redundant. I remember sitting in the meeting room sobbing in front of them while they told me I no longer had a job and I questioned my worth. I felt like a total failure, full of embarrassment and shame.

Looking back now I know they did me a favour. I should have walked away before that because I now realise I was worth so much more. I did have the skills and I did have the knowledge to manage that spa; they were the ones that had the issue and it was projected on to me. However, other things began to break down in my personal life and I then decided that I just needed to get away and realign.

## New adventures can be the making of you

I needed to start a new chapter in my life, so my friend and I met up and planned our trip around the world. We set off from Heathrow airport, our first stop being Thailand, then on to Fiji and finally Australia. We had the best time and I'm so thankful I got to travel with my friend and share so many amazing experiences together.

I then decided I wanted to venture on to New Zealand and America. So I set myself up as a solo traveller. It was scary going off by myself, I only had myself to depend on and the thought of not having anyone by my side was a daunting one.

The trip ended up being the making of me. I conquered my fears of travelling solo and I chose to believe that I could travel alone and still have an amazing time. Travelling changed me as a person; it made me have a totally different outlook on life and it opened my eyes that I really can do anything I set out to achieve.

## Self-belief creates success

Fast forward to now and I am a multi award-winning salon owner with employees and a team of self-employed therapists within my business. I made a profit in my first year and have gone from strength to strength ever since.

I didn't ever believe I would get this far because I didn't believe in myself all those years ago. There have been occasions where I've listened to others who would bring me down, but if I had continued to listen to them then I would have never taken all those leaps in life and be where I am now. I wouldn't be sitting here writing this chapter about inspirational women in business. It's hard to believe I am one of those inspirational women!

There will always be moments in my life where my self-belief will start to fade, but it's important when that happens to look back and see all the other times that I have changed my mindset and I have succeeded. When you want something badly enough, there is no other option; your determination will come naturally when you believe in yourself.

It's really sad to think that some people will never believe in themselves enough and they will always stay in their comfort zone. Comfort zones are totally fine for some people, but as an entrepreneur that won't get us to where we want to be. The same as when we doubt ourselves: we won't move forward and we will just stay in that rut being miserable and not progress to our fullest potential.

So to finish off I want you to know something very important. Firstly, you need to believe in yourself. Always trust the journey you're on, and remember that all journeys have some bumps in the road, but they are there as a lesson and development for our future. Never let anyone bring you down or question your self-worth because you are amazing and you can do anything you put your mind to.

If you have a dream then I want you to take the first step today to work towards that dream, no matter how big or small.

When you believe in yourself, magic starts to happen.

## Beccy Smart

Beccy Smart is the founder of Forever Beautiful, an award-winning skin and beauty clinic based in an old bank in the quaint small town of Wooler, Northumberland.

Although originally from the south-east (Kent), Beccy set up her business in Northumberland where her parents grew up.

Having achieved a 2.1 BA Hons in Business Management, Beccy then went on to achieve a postgraduate Certificate in Education which led her to train others who had a passion for beauty.

Beccy loves adventures and travelling the world. She is also passionate about helping others which led her to one of her greatest achievements: trekking the Great Wall of China to raise money for Macmillan Cancer Support after losing her aunty to the illness.

Beccy is best described as kind, loving and hard-working, and she enjoys spending time with family and friends.

www.forever-beautiful.co.uk

www.facebook.com/ForeverBeautifulNorthumberland

www.instagram.com/foreverbeautifulnorthumberland

# CHAPTER 5:

## Dr Bridget Kirsop

I had a dream.

And it was a big dream.

And it created my business and life success.

Dreams are from our unconscious mind, which is in charge of our emotions and behaviours – very helpful.

I was due to give a talk at a business growth event, and I had left it a bit late to plan. I had been interrupted that day by a decluttering person who had come to help me tidy my paperwork and office. So I went to sleep, thinking that I'd write my talk the next day and that was when I had the dream.

In my dream, my paperwork started flying around, my clothes swirled around my wardrobe, and it all combined to produce a whirlwind which eventually led to me sitting on a pavement. It was cold, raining and dark and I looked around and thought, I'm homeless. I had a duffel bag and a torn raincoat with me. I emptied out the duffle bag, interested to see what was inside it. There was a dog lead but no dog – Toto had left for warmer places and happier people. I had a bottle of a clear fluid which was nearly empty and was probably gin. Goodness, I couldn't remember drinking that. I had some old slippers which had got wet from the night before – and nothing else!

I had no friends, nowhere to go and no one to talk to – *I felt as though I'd lost myself.*

## I had a pretty empty bag

But it wasn't always like this.

A year before, I had been a doctor – 24 years as a GP, a Medical Director for six years, and had a seriously important and interesting job. I was respected, well known and I followed the rules. My family knew what I did and it was something that people understood. Some people would say that *I had a pretty full bag.* However, I was bored and felt frustrated and wasn't doing what I really wanted to do. I felt unfulfilled. *I wasn't being myself.*

I was lucky enough to have some coaching so that I could do a good job at being a Medical Director. The coaching completely changed my perspective on my life and my purpose. *The bag was filling up.*

So I left general practice and medicine and also left my husband who wasn't really interested in who I was. I took early retirement and *worked on who I wanted to be.*

What next? I asked myself. I could sit in the garden, by the river, and do some gardening, read, socialise and relax, but then the next thought was that I'd be unfulfilled. I thought about what had helped me to be happy and fulfilled and had helped me to create my life as I wanted – of course it was the coaching. At a deeper level, it was also about me enjoying every minute of every day and making a difference. So I started to do a life coaching qualification and then came across Neuro-Linguistic Programming – NLP. I was amazed by the thought of being able to be in charge of my life rather than blaming other people. I still feel goosebumps when I think about my NLP Practitioner course and the journey I took after that.

## I had started discovering myself and was filling up the bag again

However, this journey was very different from the journey I had been on as a GP and Director in the NHS.

- People didn't understand why I had left a secure and respected job with a good pension. My friends weren't sure what I was doing and started to move away from me – I think it was because I wasn't doing what they understood or could help with.

- I started to feel as though I wasn't good enough and I doubted myself. I felt as though I was a fraud and that success in this new career was too difficult. I still remember sitting in my office, trying to create a website, and worrying that my new husband would leave me because of the time the business was taking up.

- I was also trying to prepare a pitch for a networking event, as when I had stood up and talked the week before, my knees wobbled, my voice didn't work and I had to sit down without saying anything.

All in all, my confidence went down and I ended up on the equivalent of the pavement with no hope.

## I had lost myself again; the bag was empty

Going back to the dream (or was it the reality?), I nearly thought about ending it all. And then I saw a person walking along the road towards me. She was holding a pile of books, and when she got to me she handed me one. It was called *The Big Leap*. She looked at me and said, 'You don't look as though you belong on the street,' and then asked me this one question: 'Who do you need to be to get out of this situation? Have a think.'

I found a place to read the book. It was fascinating. I realised that I had been getting in my own way and that the question of "Who did I need to be?" was the right question. To add to the question: "Who was I now and what was I doing that stopped me from being the person I wanted to be?" It was such a profound thought that *the bag shook in agreement*.

I stood up and threw away the bottle!

The rain stopped and I walked towards a warm room and continued reading the book.

Toto the dog returned with some of her friends and people started talking to me on the street. They wanted to know what I'd learned that had made such a difference to how I behaved and my confidence levels.

## Lessons from the bag

As a result of the amazing Big Dream, I have concepts that I now help people with to enable them to be successful in business.

## First lesson out of the bag

Business (and Life) Success = Total Clarity + Total Belief + massive and consistent action

Definitions:

- Success is whatever that means to you
- Clarity is about who you are and what you want to achieve
- Belief is in yourself and what you are doing
- Massive and consistent action is what you do to get you the success that you want and deserve

## Second lesson out of the bag

Change happens at a variety of levels.

Robert Dilts has a model known as neurological levels which I teach in my NLP trainings and use in coaching with people in business. It is based on the premise that change happens at a variety of levels and I'd like to give you an insight into these levels:

**Environment:** Being clear about what the impact of the environment is in terms of people and your surroundings.

**Behaviour:** Behaving in a way that gets you success – having habits and being aware of your behaviours so you become the person that you want to be. The person you become comes from the behaviours and habits that you use.

**Skills and competencies:** Having skills and competencies to get what you want – we often have all of the resources inside of us that we need and often don't use them. So either resurrect them or learn some new ones.

**Values and beliefs:** Knowing what is important to you. My business values are:

1. Determination
2. Self-care
3. Fun
4. Making a difference

My empowering beliefs are:

- I am good enough
- I make a difference to other people
- I am in charge of my life
- I can be who I want to be

**Identity:** Knowing who you are.

**Purpose:** Knowing what our purpose for being on the planet is.

## I filled up my bag

I worked out my purpose – to enjoy every moment of every day.

I know my identity – an unsticker and a fun-lover.

I have empowering beliefs and know my values for my business.

I use my NLP skills to help others and to live the best life that I can.

I have habits and behaviours that support my identity and purpose.

I keep my boundaries in terms of other people and the environment that I work in.

## So, my bag is full

It's been an interesting journey which was started by the dream.

I now have a successful NLP training and coaching business working with business people who feel stuck and are self-sabotaging. I am the only NLP Master Trainer in Wales and feel proud of my training and coaching. And I'm having fun!

If you want to be successful you can choose to follow your own dream, fill up your own bag and be the person that you want to be. You are worth it!

Let me know if you need any help.

# Dr Bridget Kirsop

Dr Bridget is a former GP and Medical Director. She felt as though she was only scratching the surface of the causes of poor health and so she left the NHS.

The NLP coaching she experienced during her role inspired her to train as an NLP coach and NLP Master Trainer – one of the few in the UK. She remembers vividly the huge changes from her training and they have stayed with her.

She works with people in business who self-sabotage and she helps them to make massive differences to their profit and alignment with their business.

She is quirky and passionate and enjoys every minute of every day.

She lives in Wales with her pets. She regularly undertakes her administration in the chicken run and has a very stubborn and opinionated English Bull Terrier – a joy to live with!

info@drbridgetnlp.com

www.drbridgetnlp.com

www.facebook.com/groups/onestepcloserwithdrbridget

www.instagram.com/drbridgetcoach

www.linkedin.com/in/drbridgetnlp

INSPIRATIONAL WOMEN OF THE WORLD

# CHAPTER 6:

## Christina Taylor-Chisholm

---

### Fall in love with sales: learn how to sell

Sales is the backbone of any business. Without sales, you don't have a business. I believe that anyone can learn the sales process and fall in love with sales, even if they hate selling. I know this because that is exactly what happened to me.

Back in the late 90s, I was at Newcastle college studying art and design. I was working as a receptionist at the weekends, and I'd just taken on a telesales job three nights a week to support myself through college. I didn't have a clue how to sell, but how hard could it be? At least that's what I thought until I started. I was put on the home movers' team, and after my initial training my job was to take inbound calls from people wanting to move house and make outbound calls to sell BT products. After my first few days, I absolutely hated it!

When people called to move house, I'd complete their order and get off the phone as quickly as possible. Outbound calling was even worse. People would shout at you, slam the phone down on you and one guy even asked what colour knickers I was wearing when he answered! I was at the point where I was tired, miserable and depressed. I was completely shattered from being at college all day and working two jobs and I knew I needed to do something to improve the quality of my life. Although I didn't like the telesales job, the wages were far better than my receptionist's job. Also, the hatred of the job wasn't the same story for everyone. Some of the salespeople were earning *huge* bonuses and seemed to really enjoy their job.

That's when I had my lightbulb moment. *If I learned how to sell, I'd be able to leave my other job, get my weekends back, not be as exhausted and earn more money than I was currently earning.* But how the hell could I learn to sell?

I bought numerous sales books and spent my evenings devouring the contents. I also started shadowing the top sellers in the centre, taking lots of notes so that I could implement the same techniques they were using. Most importantly, I needed to change my mindset. Instead of dreading going into work, I visualised how I'd feel if I could leave my receptionist's job, get my weekends back, have more money, more energy, and enjoy my sales job. I put into practice everything I'd learned from the sales books and the top sellers…

1. I started following the sales process.

2. I was enthusiastic on every call.

3. I started talking more to my customers, building up a rapport with them.

4. I would ask them lots of open questions so I could present the correct solution.

5. I would upsell on *every* single call.

6. I would objection handle every concern that was thrown at me.

7. I would take as many calls as I could on my shift to maximise sales opportunities.

8. I stopped letting rejection bother me and accepted this was just part of the process.

Did my efforts pay off? Absolutely! After just a couple of weeks I'd taken hundreds of phone calls, stayed consistent and maximised every single opportunity. Sales (and my bonus!) were through the roof. I had achieved my goal. Leaving my other job and getting my weekends back felt bloody amazing too. Not only that, but I was also really enjoying my job and the process. Not long after that, I was offered a job as a sales coach to help other people learn how to sell too. From there I went on to be a sales trainer, then sales manager, using the skills I'd learned to help hundreds of people along the way.

## Create the life you want

The truth is that it is up to *you* to create the life that you desire. Greatness exists inside all of us, and in my experience, it is only when you truly understand yourself, your skills, your passion, your values and what drives you as a person that you can achieve great success.

Fast forward a couple of years and I'm now married (to a salesman, obviously!), working as a project manager on some of the company's biggest deals. I was working 60-hour weeks, away from home, often flying internationally with work at a moment's notice. It was hard work, but I was making a name for myself. It all seemed so important until… I fell pregnant! At that moment, everything changed. I'd changed. I no longer wanted to work away from home, I wanted to be at home. When my daughter was born, that feeling only intensified. I wanted to spend as much time as I could at home with my family.

The thought of leaving my daughter and working away from home again left me feeling anxious. *That's when I decided to change my life. I would leave my old job and set up my own business, using all the skills I'd learned along the way. I'd work my own hours and spend lots of time with my family.* But what business would I set up?

I wrote down a list of all my skills, hobbies, things that I'd enjoyed doing in my life, and also the hours I wanted to work. I knew that if I was going to change my life, I was going to do something I really enjoyed.

That's when Popolo Ceramico was born!

After my daughter's birth, I'd found it difficult finding personalised ceramics that were not only great keepsakes but also incredibly stylish, so made great gifts and looked fabulous in the home. I was also very creative, so I knew I'd be able to produce some awesome designs. I rented space in the local pottery, working alongside some of the north east's leading ceramicists to learn my trade.

My products proved to be a huge success and my business really started to take off. The truth is, building a successful business doesn't happen overnight. It takes lots of planning, hard work and resilience. You need to be passionate about your product, you need to know if there is a market for it, understand who your ideal client is, and knowing your numbers is essential to build a successful business.

A couple of years later, I welcomed my second child into the world, and I kept my business at a manageable level so I could spend lots of time with my family. Product demand was growing though, and I knew that the only way to grow my business effectively would be through franchising. I knew that my proven business model, paired with my sales training experience, would be a winning combination. Once both children were in school, I enlisted my first franchisee and since then we have taken on over 20 franchisees within the UK, we have launched an online range and we'll soon be launching in Australia. I know that you can change your life and create the life you wish for if you want it badly enough and if you are willing to put the work in.

## Never stop growing

I believe you should never stop growing as a person. If you find something that you are good at and that you are passionate about, then you'll never work a day in your life. I am passionate about helping people achieve their goals and creating more sales within their businesses, which is why I also work as a sales speaker, coach and trainer as well as leading my own franchise network.

The truth is that we become who we hang around with, so make friends with people who are growing and learning. As they achieve new things, it will inspire you to want to achieve new things too.

I am very fortunate that I have an incredibly good friend who has a very similar mindset to mine. She is also a franchisor and works as a speaker too. We were chatting one day about how difficult it was finding speakers that specifically targeted small and medium enterprises. That's when we decided to set up a business together. We were friends, we both had a background in business, a similar mindset and we had spotted a gap in the market. We decided to set up The Inspirational Speaker Agency, a speaker agency specifically for the SME market. It's our new project and it's great to be working with another entrepreneur as we have already learned so much from each other.

One thing I have learned is to focus on one thing at a time and don't try and do everything yourself. I have various businesses now, therefore it would be impossible for me to manage them all without the correct team in place. Finally, and the most important takeaway I can give you today is to *learn to love sales*. This is one skill that you'll use throughout your life.

# Christina Taylor-Chisholm

Christina Taylor-Chisholm is a multiple award-winning entrepreneur. She is the franchisor at Popolo Ceramico Ltd, co-founder of the Inspirational Speaker Agency Ltd and a sales coach, trainer and speaker. Christina is passionate about helping people to see their full potential and achieve their goals. She believes that anyone can learn to fall in love with sales.

Christina has worked in sales for over 20 years. She started as a telesales advisor within BT Group and she was soon the top seller within her division. She was then promoted to sales coach, trainer, then manager before becoming a project manager.

After the birth of her daughter, Christina set up Popolo Ceramico, then went on to franchise the business to help other individuals who wanted to work flexibly around their families. Sales has always been her passion and she now helps other people make more sales within their businesses.

www.facebook.com/groups/901459137178411

www.instagram.com/christinasalessuperstar

www.linkedin.com/in/christina-taylor-chisholm-b1260439

# CHAPTER 7:

## Christine Marsh

---

### Expectations vs Reality: Building Blocks

In the business world, branding is an accepted marketing essential. However, I had no choice of my name, but was given an identity and individuality. It includes my self-awareness and self-esteem.

I had to overcome external judgment calls from birth. My father had ordered a son, William Richard. Perhaps I was a rebel from conception? There was a trade description discrepancy between his expectations and the reality of who was delivered. He never used the name on my birth certificate, Christine Elizabeth. Instead, I became 'A Girl Named Bill'.

I became a mascot for his boxing team, and witnessed the damage caused by competition where defeat was the measure of success. I was splattered with blood while watching grown men smash hell out of each other while seated at the ringside.

I decided there had to be another option and have always advocated the benefits of collaboration and community spirit. Hence my commitment to creating allies, not opponents.

Because of the constant moves, and due to my father's military postings, my education was disrupted. Nevertheless, I managed two consecutive years at an excellent grammar school and obtained the required certificates. As a girl, university was not an option. I was allowed to go to art college. Then I was expected to get 'a proper job' and joined the Civil Service.

Growing up, I conformed to the orthodox female roles of a daughter, sister, wife and mother. After my nomadic childhood, I did want a stable home life and family. Therefore, my husband's redundancy came as a shock. In the 1970s, this situation was not such a common occurrence. With a mortgage to pay and two young daughters, it proved to be the trigger for me to start earning some pocket money to help.

I became the village Avon lady; I never thought of it as 'selling'. I was helping a customer make an informed decision.

Then a multi-level marketing opportunity arose and we joined, lured by the promise of making a lot of money by motivational masters. I couldn't see the point in selling small quantities to households and instead focused on business sales.

I was appointed Regional Manager for distributors in the south-west of England. Achieving the best sales results resulted in speaking at an international conference in Geneva. I have an innate naivety. I didn't know I couldn't, so I just did it anyway.

Life-altering events have become an accepted part of life's rich pattern.

Change is inevitable. Stress is manageable. Misery is optional.

All experiences should be valued, no matter whether seen as apparently random or a setback. When facing a major change, I picture myself carrying a bindle stick with my mementoes wrapped in a red spotted hanky. Before any move, I assess the contents and only keep what serves and motivates me.

My philosophy is based on:

"Simplicity is the ultimate sophistication." – Leonardo Da Vinci

"I am not what happened to me. I am what I choose to become." – Carl Gustav Jung

## University of Life: Multi-faceted Career

Nobody expected me to seek a career, least of all myself. It just evolved. There were shock waves when I had a late teenage rebellion and stopped trying to match other people's expectations. I decided to explore; who was this woman called Christine?

Risk in business goes with accepting personal responsibility for decisions. My initial challenge had been proving to myself that I had the 'ability' to respond! Playing down one's talents is a fairly common female trait. External judgment calls are based on other people's experiences and the opinions they have formed.

I changed my mindset from looking at certain business environments as being 'male dominated' to being 'predominately male' as a snapshot at this point in time. I saw it as choosing between the best available talent, rather than as discrimination against me. I wanted to be judged by whether I was good at what I did.

I had to start somewhere seeking a 'proper job', I did the rounds of local recruitment agencies. I was deemed to be unemployable as I had no vocational qualifications. One lady encouraged me to take credit for what I had achieved, and helped unpack the contents of my red spotted hanky! Art college and sales experience came together.

Selling newspaper advertising space meant I was selling a promise! In order that my customers would be able to measure a return on their investment, we set up a tracking process. Based on results, I was promoted to Sales Representative.

I approached a local farmer, who had started a company providing quality meat to freezer owners. What did I know about meat? I only knew how to cook mince, chops, blade of lamb and fillet steak on special occasions. I sold myself to become Sales Manager. Sales were trebled in 18 months by trying new ways of spreading the word of the excellent products, and providing a reliable delivery service.

When a national freezer company opened branches locally, I could see incredible opportunities to increase their frozen meat sales. To me the core principles were the same, or similar; I wasn't daunted by the difference in turnover. It was simply a matter of where the decimal point was!

When researching, I found only job opportunities for females within the traditional roles. I'd learned not to be daunted by the status quo and retained my childlike belief that anything is possible. If there wasn't a job, I'd have to create one!

I wrote a letter to the Marketing Director requesting 46 minutes of his time as I had ideas that would increase their sales. Fortunately, he was a betting man and accepted my suggestion to mitigate any risk by agreeing a three-month trial. This opened up incredible opportunities, resulting in holding senior management roles in Operational, Learning & Development and HR.

I'd found my niche – the ability to create a link between a supplier's expertise, their goods and/or services and match these to the needs of their internal and external customers.

The founding of Prime Objectives was a leap of faith based on the belief that I had something of value to offer that would be more effective as an external resource, serving companies of all disciplines, shapes and sizes.

In addition to my own clients, adhering to genuine collaboration with respected associates has given me the opportunity to gain incredible experience within large international organisations. I was open to learning about the field of performance improvement, I had the opportunity to expand my knowledge, travel to many countries and present at international conferences.

## Focus on the Future: The Way Forward

The world pandemic has served as a wakeup call, whilst demolishing my life as I knew it. However, I'm not afraid to start over. This time I'm not starting from scratch. Knowledge comes from learning. Wisdom comes from experience. Life is a continuous learning curve. What is fact today is fiction tomorrow.

I only know what I know at any given point in time with the amazing capacity to embrace personal growth and seek new adventures. I've learned to get in the flow by doing what I love and enjoying a state of mind in which everything is possible and unstoppable.

When ahead of the crowd with new ideas, it can be lonely if you are in a majority of one! I've always trusted my inner vision, and haven't let others change my mind. It is my life anyway! To reach a tipping point, you need to build up from a few supporters to reach the critical mass required to implement a new venture successfully.

What is my brand? Focusing on the future, I will embrace that I am a medicine woman and healer: ensuring creating allies not opponents.

"Angels will catch your feet and provide the stepping stones as you walk out into the void of the unknown."

My vision when I started Prime Objectives back in 1990 was 'Uniting Mind, Heart and Spirit' both on a personal and business level. Spirituality had still been seen as 'woo-woo' stuff, and I had previously worked under the radar!

More businesses have had a shift in priorities to embrace spirituality in a profound way, demonstrating the quality of being concerned with the human spirit as opposed to only valuing material or physical things. I have found only a few genuine leaders who encapsulate these qualities and ethics.

"Not everything that matters can be measured and not everything that can be measured matters." – Albert Einstein

I have shared with you some of my stories, the lessons I've learned and achievements which may resonate with you. I am reaching out to kindred spirits, who share similar ideals and values and are open to exploring the new opportunities that are relevant today.

"Logic gets you from A to B. Imagination will take you anywhere."
– Albert Einstein

# Christine Marsh

Christine Marsh, Prime Objectives, is a respected facilitator and change agent dedicated to creating allies, not opponents, and ensuring positive progress.

Christine has extensive experience working with different business disciplines, both in the public and private sectors, across many cultures. She researches, designs and delivers customised focus sessions and workshops. Her creative, pragmatic approach identifies the core issues to be resolved.

Christine's ability to understand complex situations is based on her successful career within a multi-million dollar retail environment. She held senior management roles spanning Operations and Learning & Development.

Christine is an inspirational and thought-provoking speaker. She has experience speaking internationally and to membership groups.

Christine led a nomadic life due to her father's various military postings. Born in India, educated in Singapore and the UK, she has retained her love of global travel, and is always open to experiencing new adventures.

www.linkedin.com/in/christinemarshcpt

www.youtube.com/c/ChristineMarshCPT

www.facebook.com/ChristineMarshSpeaks

INSPIRATIONAL WOMEN OF THE WORLD

# CHAPTER 8:

## Dawn Evans

---

### Diversification through a pandemic

Successful people know that they are capable of making the right decisions for their lives to find the success that they seek. They see something that is a great opportunity, or they come up with a brilliant idea, and they take action to turn that vision into a reality.

Well, action is what I took back in 2006, when I was working as a leisure centre manager and a part-time college lecturer whilst being a devoted wife and raising two young children. I decided to take the plunge into entrepreneurship and start a training business. People around me questioned my sanity, especially three years later when I gave up my stable job for my 'hobby business'. It's hard work turning your vision into a reality, and something most people will not put the time and effort in to making it happen. But happen it did and 14 years and one global pandemic later, my business is thriving and stronger than ever, along with my five other companies and growing property portfolio.

So, let's focus on the pandemic. March 23rd 2020. The day my company halted, and the day we all now know as 'The day lockdown began'. I remember it well; business was booming, the diary was full, we had around 50 courses booked in for the next two weeks. The government made their announcement ordering people to 'Stay at Home'. Well, that wasn't good for business when I was running a training academy, relying on my classrooms to be full of students to give me an income. The phone began to ring, cancellation after cancellation, until my healthy-looking diary was completely empty. Not a course in sight. I looked across the office to my operations manager, Ruth; Ruth looked back at me, both wondering what the hell we were going to do. I had two choices that day: to sit and wallow in self-pity crying poor me, or to put my thinking cap on and come up with a plan that would protect me, my staff and my business. I chose the latter.

I remember ringing my good friend Tracey that evening and asking her what she was going to do, as she also had a service-based company. Everything got cancelled for her as well. I said there must be hundreds of women in our situation; our conversation quickly turned from what we could do to how we were going to help others in our situation. We decided to open a Facebook group, to help, encourage, uplift and inspire other women. This group grew very quickly, and within a few months we had 6,000 women join us from 80 different countries. WOW! In fact, IWOW is what I named our group, short for Inspirational Women of the World. It became a safe space for women to talk through the pandemic, to help, guide, support and lift each other up when needed.

It soon turned into a company, and an online network and membership was created, followed by a retreat in the beautiful Forest of Dean, and a multi-author book was created which became an Amazon No 1 Best Seller. In fact, it is the first book in what is now our inspirational series; this book you are reading is book two. We also planned a trip to Morocco, which will happen in May 2022. All in all, a great success during the pandemic, my first example of diversification through a pandemic.

Meanwhile back at the company HQ of Ajuda, the training academy was still closed, face to face training was non-existent, as were the clients. I needed to act fast here too, in order to save the company that I had been building for the past 14 years.

I called a staff meeting, got my team together and said we need to take our training online, and within weeks I had created two Zoom accounts, retrained our instructors to facilitate online delivery, contacted all our clients to inform them they had an option of completing the training course online, and then away we went. Three weeks later, while the world stood still, I was up and running once again, doing what I do best, educating people to save lives, which is also the strapline of my training company Ajuda.

The one thing that you need to have if you want to be successful is self-confidence, with a clear vision and belief in your ability to lead. Yes, things will get tough, but we women are made of pure toughness, and the quick thinking not only saved my training company but my events company too. Prior to the pandemic I was due to host the city's largest Mental Health & Wellbeing Show. I had the local stadium booked, all my speakers in place, 40 of them, several exhibitors confirmed, and worst of all 1,462 tickets sold to delegates!

Once again, my research started. I began googling online events companies, IT companies, and then came across virtual reality expos. Is this even a thing? I asked myself. Well, yes it was, and £18,000 later I had bought a virtual reality platform and shifted my whole event online. It was a great success. So much so, we have continued to run monthly mental health webinars, on a variety of topics relating to mental health and wellbeing, which are attended by 400-600 delegates each month. And great news, we are back live in May 2022, even bigger and better. The Lord Mayor has offered to open the show, we have members of the Senedd (Welsh Parliament) delivering talks, along with all major charities, such as Samaritans, BEAT, Bipolar UK, Stonewall, Action for Children and many more, and we have secured Frank Bruno as our headline speaker.

I could have given up during the pandemic, but not only did I push through, but I also diversified to survive, and survive and thrive is what I did.

So, in summary, things will get hard from time to time, you will have setbacks and challenges, but it's how you deal with those challenges that will either make or break you. Know your own ability, focus on what needs to be done; once you decide the way forward, set realistic goals, communicate well, work hard and believe in yourself.

If you don't believe that you can accomplish anything, then you won't. If you don't make that change, then the chances are that you will continue to do what you have always done, and if you don't diversify, you may end up in trouble financially or mentally, and end up just existing, not living. Make the impossible a possibility by taking action – after all, if you separate the word impossible, it says 'I'm possible'. If you have faith in your ideas, opinions and abilities, you will be able to accomplish your goals, even if circumstances lead you to diversify. Have faith in your ability to lead the life you've always dreamed of having.

There is a great saying by Richard Branson: "You need to work a few years like other people won't, so you can live many years like other people can't." I really love this quote, and it is so true, and that is what I have done, and if you find a job that you truly love, you will never work another day in your life.

The other thing that the pandemic has taught me is that there is more than one way to diversify. I want to share this with you in the hope that it will help you in your business too:

- Concentric Diversification

- Horizontal Diversification

- Conglomerate Diversification

- Vertical Diversification

And lastly, I would like to share the importance of having multiple income streams. Again, when the income from my training company dropped during the pandemic, so did the price of commercial property, so much so that I bought the office block next door to our training centre for 50% of the original asking price. There are opportunities everywhere, you just need to look for them and be ready to bounce when they come knocking. As a coach I always tell my clients to have at least five income streams, the average millionaire will have seven, one being property and the others some kind of investment. This will ensure that your bucket will never run dry.

Talking about buckets, imagine you have seven dripping taps flowing into a bucket, and two turn off. This happened for real, as I mentioned above. I was always going to be OK, even without the diversification that I mentioned, as I have five more taps still flowing into that bucket. So, ask yourself – how many taps have you got filling your bucket?

In summary, don't be scared to try new things in life and in business, to diversify, change direction, start on a new path if and when needed, as the journey is just as important as the destination.

I hope this chapter has helped you in your journey through entrepreneurship and diversification following the pandemic.

# Dawn Evans

With 15 years of business experience, numerous awards and qualifications, Dawn knows what she is doing when it comes to female entrepreneurship. Just before the pandemic she was socialising with billionaire Sir Richard Branson on his private island. She regularly speaks on large stages to global audiences on her business growth strategies.

Dawn is CEO of multi-award-winning vocational training company Ajuda Ltd, founder of Wales' biggest ever education and mental health shows, owner of Ajuda Property Management Ltd, co-founder of Inspirational Women of the World (IWOW Ltd) and a published children's author. All have given her vast skills and experience as a successful entrepreneur. Dawn specialises in motivating, inspiring and developing startup and growing business. With degrees in Education, Sustainable Leadership and Coaching & Mentoring for Entrepreneurial Practice, she uses these qualifications and puts them into practice to develop and create new entrepreneurs of the future.

dawn@ajuda.org.uk

www.ajudacoachingacademy.org.uk

www.twitter.com/ajudadawn

# CHAPTER 9:

## Francess

---

### Time to create Heaven on Earth

Happiness and success are not excess cortisol stress hormones, it is time to end all abuse.

#### Presence

Today is our present

Our present is a present

Only if and when we are present

And can be pleasant

Life is God's gift.

I believe joy in our work is both possible and optimal by living in accord with God's spirit of Love. It is certainly true that 'by their fruits we know them and blessed are the peacemakers for they are all children of God.' Let us remember God is Love.

I believe we are more successful working fewer hours in order to give our home and family more quality time. In recent decades, the demands on mothers are huge. The relentless demands of work and family tear at a mother's heart and mind, creating great anxiety for her and her child/children. Our family and children must come first, for the stability of our children's health and wellbeing as well as the wellbeing of our family. We must recognise that men need respect and purpose too.

I believe work does not need to be so demanding and stressful. Work can operate at a comfortable and manageable pace with great quality of life. With dedication, hard work, trust and faith, your business will grow naturally.

**Stress** is very fashionable in this modern work world, yet stress is the primary cause of sickness and ill health, both mental and physical. Stress is not a positive health or career choice, even though it is in vogue and strongly marketed. Stress is unsustainable and creates fears, insecurities and dependency, sometimes with unhealthy addictions.

I know life is designed to be pleasant and I know work can be wonderful if we adhere to keeping a healthy work-life balance. This includes looking after you.

I know we can create *Heaven on Earth* when we truly work in accord with our passions and talents for helping and serving others joyfully and kindly. When we fully walk in Spirit, life is wonderful.

## Via Veritas Vita

Only 'The truth will set you free.' (John 8:32)

The truth is our only way to freedom from stress and insecurities inside of us. The truth is that *Faith* is a psychology of and for the most positive thought process. Faith is not a specific doctrine or religion, but a way of thinking for the positive mindset of hope and confidence in the future. Faith is defined by Hebrews 11:1 as 'The assured expectation of the things hoped for, the evident demonstration of realities not yet beheld.' Faith is the ultimate Positive Psychology for a successful and good outcome in any situation. Faith is a mental discipline needed as our natural inclination is towards fear and doubt. Doubt loses confidence and self-worth which are positive qualities we need to achieve and be successful in all aspects of our life.

*Our thoughts are Creative*, and the truth is we create what we think. So, it is vitally important to keep our thoughts positive with faith for the optimum outcome of health, happiness, wellbeing and success in all aspects of life.

## Happiness

Jesus Christ says, 'There is more happiness in giving than there is in receiving' (Acts 20:35).

Robert Holden of The Happiness Project and Success Intelligence says, 'We do not become happy because we are successful; we become successful because we are happy.'

If we are happy in what we do every day, then we are happy in our lives. This to me is real success. Happiness begins at home, in our childhood, and so to have a strong home presence is vitally important for our children and all our futures.

When we are stressed, our rational and thinking frontal cortex of our brain is shut off as this is what the well-known adrenal 'fight, flight, freeze syndrome' does. This is our body's autonomic nervous system's sympathetic response to fearful or stressful situations and may cause problems like food intolerance, allergies, anxieties, panic attacks and heart palpitations. In order to be conscious and free thinking with the power of reason, we must be comfortable and relaxed. Stress inhibits conscious free thinking and causes mistakes, unreasonableness and conflict with self and others.

**Time** is an elusive stress which is more beneficial when thought of as a whole and complete process to complete a task. When we are stressed, there is not enough time because adrenalin runs out. Time is eternal, with trust and faith employed as conscious states of being. Life could be optimal for mothers and their children with school hours from perhaps 10am. A relaxed morning with quality time for our children, a good breakfast with time, and no traffic jams.

## Health

You must look after you, you must look after your health and wellbeing as we look after our family and customers.

You must value yourself as well as others, and of course all in respect to the greatest source of Love and Light, our Heavenly Father God, who is Love.

You must value what you do, otherwise how else can anyone value you?

**Kinesiology** is a wonderful way to find the truths causing stress in our body. These truths will be known to you, though not always conscious.

Often a painful experience needs to be mourned and tears may come. Tears are often a part of the grieving process and they do come and go. Holding back grief may give rise to the grief taking a physical manifestation such as depression or other labelled diseases. But only 'the truth sets you free' ( John 8:32) and as Jesus Christ says, 'Blessed are those who mourn for they will be comforted' (Matthew 5:4). Grieving is a healing process, I know this to be true.

God has a promise 'to wipe away every tear from our eyes and death will be no more, neither will mourning nor outcry nor pain be anymore. The former things have passed away' (Revelation 21:4).

James 2:26 says, 'Our body without spirit is dead just as faith without works is dead.' Life only comes from attaining the fullness and the Oneness of The Whole Spirit of Love Anointed which is the meaning of The Most High name, Jesus Christ (Philippians 2:9). This is how we attain to The Holy Spirit of Peace, when we can reach The One place of Love within our body, The Temple where God's Love does dwell.

It is impossible to attain the spiritual state of the fullness and wholeness of Peace and Love when stressed, hence #Loveisnotacortisol stress hormone. Stress hormones come from unkindness like bullying, abuse, betrayal, lies and corruption causing hurts, grief and pain. So, at 'the last trumpet' we can and will be 'changed just as in the twinkling of an eye' as our governing rules are raised from corruptible to incorruptible (I Corinthians 15:51), and we will walk by Spirit.

Good living with peace, joy and happiness creates naturally strong immune systems. These come from good, strong family values of moral love, good care, good education, good foods, healthy relationships and artistic expression via the arts of writing, art, dance and music. Also physical fitness through sports, with healthy friendships for positive connections creating naturally occurring endorphins in our blood for *Heaven on Earth*.

**The End**: Revelation 21:5

The end is the beginning of the word endorphin

The end of the quest for heart smiles in Love

Mimicked by opium posing as opiates

Killing pain, knowing pleasure, addictive

Seductive, seducing, The Lie.

The End: ending enslavement to cortisols crying for the end

The End: the release of our natural endorphins

The dopamine, the serotonin, the oxytocin, the anandamide

Binding our blood in marriage with Love

Which is always positive.

Our natural endorphins are The End to suffering.

The End is the beginning of The Word endorphin

His Love in our blood.

The End is the beginning of His promise

The End is the beginning of God's Love embodied in us

'For look, I am making all things new'

Come, Lord Jesus Christ, Come…

May the conscious understanding of God's Love come to be, for ending stress, trauma and abuse; for creating a wonderful positive life with confidence and faith in each and every day for us, for our children and our children's children for Heaven on Earth. Thanks be to God. *Love is the energy vibration and frequency of our Hu, our Light.*

Jesus Christ said in Luke 19:40: 'The stones will cry out', and he asks when he comes again, will he find the faith on Earth? (Luke 18:8).

So I write in good faith with Love for Light and #Loveisnotacortisol. Amen

My books:

*Healing Poems for Positive Love*

*Parousia Love's Light*

*Parousia Book of Life*

I am available for therapy sessions online, in person, and for stable visits for horses.

I am available for festivals, talks, poetry readings and workshops.

My photographs are available as prints and cards.

I run courses on Stress Management, Back Care, Neck Care, Self Help Reflex Points, Increasing Creativity and Writing Healing Poems.

# Francess

Francess is a Holistic Health and Beauty Therapist specialising in Health Kinesiology for people, horses and other animals.

Francess writes poetry and non-fiction on health, healing, scripture, prophecy and wellbeing. She explores the boundaries of love and fear in search of the resolve of abuses causing stress, trauma, grief, sickness and pain.

From Genesis to Revelation and from Stars to Starfish, her work addresses all in between to inspire love, trust and safety for justice and peace, for the fullness of the fruits of God's Spirit for creating Heaven on Earth.

When seriously broken and unwell, a vision of light appeared which brought healing and confidence to publish her work on the conscious healing process of the gemstones cited in Revelation 21. Thanks be to God, through The Whole Spirit of Love Anointed, namely Jesus Christ who is returning for healing our sick and troubled world.

www.Francess.org

www.facebook.com/positivelovefransmith

www.instagram.com/healingpoems

INSPIRATIONAL WOMEN OF THE WORLD

# CHAPTER 10:

## Helen Davies

**Daydream believer...**

Sitting in that primary school classroom, I looked out of the window and started to daydream (again), I dreamed of a world where I had become an astronaut exploring the stars or being a superhero, flying off to save the day. The world for me then was so full of wonder and curiosity. I wondered how I could become that person, school learning seemed tricky somehow despite those extra remedial classes. From an early age I was a dreamer, a helper, and knew I was different, a little awkward at times. I was a bit geeky in my own way, life and feelings seemed larger somehow for me than other people. I even knew I was queer at a very young age too, not that it mattered then as it was all about sport for me in my school years.

Wind forward a lifetime... I live in a home I love, 20 minutes from the sea, with a son I adore and two part-time kick-ass jobs, both with heart and purpose. The first is being a Clinical Director, one of the first nurses in the country to have a role which was traditionally a doctor's role, in an amazing position of privilege to help thousands of people. The second role is helping other parents who are neurodivergent, especially some who realise it because their child gets a neurodiverse diagnosis. I support parents to increase their joy, to thrive and gain strategies to use for them and their family. I have both ADHD and dyslexia, so writing this chapter is very special, as is releasing my forthcoming book *5 Steps To Lift Off*.

## Find your own way

So how did I get from being a daydreaming kid in remedial lessons to the top of my game, being a national lead and expert? I will share some of the top insights as to 'the how', the mindset that can help you and a few life hacks. The first and foremost message is *find your own way for things, you do not need to do it like anyone else*! Every time I have ignored this approach, I have paid for it! It's been a painful journey with things not always working out, leading to me being miserable too.

I worked out how to unlock my brain and potential. Being neurodivergent means your brain is wired differently; in my case my memory is a bit like Swiss cheese, lots of holes in it and I am never sure what I will or won't recall. Trying to remember things just in 'parrot fashion' like they teach in the classroom does not work for me! So, I need to make sure I create memory hooks, build up associations to things, and think more strategically. So, for example, I use mind maps to help plan my essays as I do not think sequentially. I also need to manage my energy carefully as I can pick up on others' energy a lot. Over time I learned to make sure my energy battery doesn't get drained so easily.

## Parent Thrive

As a person with ADHD I have energy like no other and it's like living three lives in one. I have harnessed this ability to its fullest and followed my dream of working with people, working up the nursing ladder, gaining a psychology and counselling degree, a postgraduate teaching qualification, becoming a qualified mentor, running action learning sets and now a coach. I get hyper focus (not all folks with ADHD do), my hyper focus has been about people. I have a big heart; I love helping people and making a difference to people's lives and this is what I get out of bed for every day. I'm on a mission to touch a million people's lives through my not-for-profit organisation Practical Wisdom.

I love being a parent coach, not because I am perfect but because I am paying forward all the help, advice and expertise that has taken years to learn, on top of a lifetime of being a nurse. I have compressed all this into my Parent Thrive course for parents who are neurodiverse. Again, the key message of *finding your own way* remains, you do not need to parent like anyone else nor run your home like others do. Sure, there are key principles like loving your child, spending time with them, teaching them about the world, but how you do this is yours to own.

Like I said, I have memory issues, so what that meant for me when my son was a toddler was that I was forever late and getting out of the door on time was like mission impossible. Oh, and my inner voice was super critical. 'Why can't I remember things?' 'Why aren't I a better parent?' 'All the other parents seem to have this organising lark down, why don't I?!' Which is why I teach other parents that they 'are good enough'. I have created 'parent swaps'. Let's swap that inner negative voice to 'I will get there'. Instead of beating yourself up, see what can be put into place to help. For me, a simple thing like having two bags, one for me and one for 'junior' which was ready to go helped loads. I also used to replenish the bag with what I had used as soon as I could, this way I didn't forget. Let's face it, if I say I will do it later I will often get distracted.

I also now know that no parent is perfect and the thought that all the other parents seem to have got things 'all sorted' is a misconception. I do a reframe when 'I get it wrong', swapping from 'I got this wrong' to 'what can I do differently next time?'. What I did learn is that being a reflective parent and a reflective practitioner is a very important ethos in nursing that I now use in every aspect of my life. Don't aim for being a perfect parent but a good enough one, take the pressure off yourself. I dealt with, and continue to monitor, and keep in check, that inner voice. I teach various techniques as to how to do that, one being to name it, so you think of it in the third person. It gives you a bit of distance and time to evaluate that inner critical voice.

Or is your inner voice trying to warn you that you are not safe? This could be about something right now or something from your past being triggered. Therefore, you need to stop and check if you need to be wary. It's important to note that voice and acknowledge it but don't follow it unless needed. Many people have experienced some form of post-traumatic stress disorder (PTSD) which can mean that the survival part of your brain gets easily triggered or stays on high alert. There is a crossover for many of being both neurodivergent and having PTSD that is beginning to become more acknowledged.

I believe we have 'five steps to lift off' where our primal survival tactics of fight, flight and freeze fully kick in. You can go up these 'steps' as situations escalate until you reach your primal response, and the more rational part of your brain reduces and even stops. Those who experience PTSD can already start at step two or even three as their primal brain and instincts can be overdeveloped. When we experience a significant event like a global pandemic, this too can also cause you to go up a step or more depending on the impact on you. In this scenario with both PTSD and a global pandemic, it can leave you with only one to two steps for everyday life before your primal response kicks in. On top of this, if you are going through a divorce or are a knackered parent then you are probably fighting every day to keep it together.

The good news is what goes up can also go down. There are things that can be done to de-escalate and go down the steps, including using other senses, using your nervous system to regulate, and developing your own toolkit, which I cover in the book *5 Steps To Lift Off* and in my Parent Thrive courses. For now, let me leave you with my top 10 life hacks.

1. Find your own way

2. Don't let perfect get in the way of being good enough

3. Keep your inner voice in check

4. Self-assess what gives you energy and what takes it away

5. Swap guilt for learning

6. You are good enough

7. Reflective parenting and life approach

8. Think how to add more joy to your day

9. Make a list daily (in your head is fine) of all the things you are grateful for

10. Play to your strengths

So, until next time remember you've got this, you do not need to do it like anyone else, find your own way.

# Helen Davies

Helen is a coach and nurse, with over 30 years of experience of working in health and wellbeing. From a child struggling at school due to her dyslexia, she has risen through the ranks to become a Clinical Director and entrepeneur.

She is a passionate champion for neurodiversity, fully aware of the challenges whilst also seeing the positive aspects too. Founder of Practical Wisdom, a not-for-profit organisation, Helen is on a mission to *touch a million lives*, ensuring individuals don't just survive but thrive. It provides online resources for neurodivergent wellbeing and in-person coaching for parents who are neurodivergent, particularly with ADHD traits. She often jokes that also having ADHD traits has meant she lives three lives at once!

Helen currently lives in the south coast of England in Sussex, enjoying kayaking, beach walks, and believing you are never too old to keep dancing like no one is watching!

www.practicalwisdom.uk

www.instagram.com/helenatpracticalwisdom

www.linkedin.com/in/helendaviesuk

INSPIRATIONAL WOMEN OF THE WORLD

# CHAPTER 11:

## Karen Newton

**Being an Entrepreneur**

Entrepreneur! The word still sends shivers down my spine. It triggers feelings of warmth, love and gratitude. Some people call me a workaholic. The truth is being an entrepreneur is a way of life, it is not something you switch on and off. It is part of who you are and I love everything about it. Freedom, choice, creativity, learning, commitment and so much more. I cannot imagine being or doing anything else.

**One Door Has to Close Before Another Can Open**

As a youngster being an entrepreneur was not part of my future plans.

I had an employee mindset, believing a job would provide me with stability. I left school at 17, joining Inland Revenue where I worked mainly in the self-employed department. Here, I learned how to read profit/loss statements and balance sheets. An indispensable skill for an entrepreneur.

When I married and moved to New Zealand, banking became the next step profession. Eastern & Central Savings Bank was a young bank, only two years old. I started the day the first ATM went into New Zealand. My job was to encourage people to use ATMs, provide them with cards and teach them how to use the machines.

Eastern & Central was ahead of the rest of the world for banking systems. It was 1982 and they were already providing automated banking. A client could deposit money into the ATM using their card, then go to the teller and the transaction already showed on their account. This was unheard of in other countries that were still operating manual ledgers.

As the bank grew, it merged with other savings banks to create Trust Bank and later Westpac Trust. As it grew, I received several promotions which saw me climb the corporate ladder, to eventually become a manager. Along the way I worked in accounting, mortgages, securities, IT, forex and visa. I loved everything about the financial industry.

One day, on my way home from work, my life changed forever.

A speeding car went through a stop sign. I couldn't brake fast enough and hit it. My car went into a somersault and was hit multiple times by surrounding vehicles. Three days later, I awoke in hospital, my body broken and battered, with the doctors telling me I would never walk again.

I had other plans.

It took two years to learn to walk. While it was a success, I had to admit a level of defeat as I was never able to gain sufficient stability within my spine and legs to play sports again.

The bank was very supportive, doing everything they could to help me get back to work; it soon became apparent though that I couldn't handle the stress of quick decision making needed for the financial markets, and had to resign.

A door closed on my perfect life.

## A Sponge

Inland Revenue and Banking taught me about money, financial markets, business systems and automation. Both also had great personal development training programmes based around soft skills such as communication and leadership.

Yet being self-employed is still a shock when you realise how little you know about the business world.

The internet was non-existent and the only way to learn was to go to university. I registered with EIT Hawkes Bay for as many courses as I could. The professors laughed and called me a professional student as I studied commercial law, accounting, business management, quality management and marketing.

My husband, Ron, had just started a business when I left banking and it seemed the most natural choice to join him. I became co-director of a fire protection company.

Ron was regarded as one of the top fire engineers in New Zealand. His incredible knowledge meant he was in high demand, travelling around New Zealand and Australia. I was left running a company with little knowledge about fire protection. Luckily, I'm a quick learner.

Very few people are ready to become entrepreneurs. Even fewer have the skills or knowledge to build a successful business. The mind needs to be like a sponge, soaking up as much information as possible to support not only business growth but personal growth.

## Accept Not Everyone Will Like You

I arrived early and found the best spot to observe the whole room. I watched him walk into the room, he saw me, turned around and walked back out. He checked the name above the room, then made a beeline for me.

This was the President of the Fire Protection Industry Contractors Association (FPICA) and for the next 10 minutes I was grilled about what right I had to be in the room.

Ron and I had been excited when we were invited to join the association. It was acceptance that our business was now one of the top fire protection companies in NZ. We had ruffled a few feathers along the way to having an 85% market share in the Hawke's Bay region, so I wasn't going to this first meeting expecting the red carpet to be rolled out.

As I sat there, being grilled about my right to be in the room, it soon became apparent that upsetting companies as we expanded our business wasn't the issue, it was simply that I was a woman. The only woman in fire protection in New Zealand, and he did not want a woman at his meeting. Throughout the meeting and for the next six months he ignored every question or comment I made. He refused to even acknowledge me at the meetings.

Things became worse when our company was voted one of the top security companies in New Zealand and we were invited to join the New Zealand Security Association. He was President. I almost didn't go to the meeting but he wasn't going to win. Attend I did. Again, he totally ignored me.

The biggest lesson I learned throughout this experience is to keep doing what you are doing if it's good for your business, but accept not everyone will like you.

## Trailblazing

After six months of being ignored by the FPICA President, the annual elections were due. I received a phone call from some members asking if I would stand for the President's position. I initially declined, but after a few more calls I accepted the nomination and won the election, becoming the first woman President of the FPICA.

The constitution required an annual election, with the President doing a maximum of two years. After my two years as President, the members approached me to change the constitution. After five years as President, I finally stepped down, proud of the changes I had instigated throughout the fire protection industry in New Zealand, Australia and Singapore.

During my Presidency we merged different associations together and brought the fire brigade and fire insurance council under one umbrella, called the New Zealand Fire Protection Association (NZFPA); we introduced industry training qualifications; all member companies became ISO9001 certified; we negotiated joint fire standards between Australia and New Zealand; we introduced fire ratings for buildings; and we moved the industry from reactive to proactive fire-fighting. We introduced automation.

During this period, our company continued to grow. It became the first company in NZ to be accredited ISO9000 for the full company. Up till that time, companies only achieved ISO for specific processes within their business. By making the whole company ISO certified we set a new benchmark for future businesses in New Zealand.

At the time we didn't realise we were trailblazers in business and fire protection. We were simply building a business and creating opportunities which would help the business continue to grow.

## An Entrepreneur

My perfect world was ripped apart following the car crash and the door was closed on my life as an employee.

The door that opened in front of me was one as an entrepreneur.

It is a tough world of ups and downs. It can be a lonely world, where you start to question your own ability. You question if you have the skills, knowledge and mental strength to survive it.

It is a world of opportunities where the only barrier to what you can achieve is your limiting beliefs.

Being an entrepreneur has challenged me to think differently. Encouraged me to dream big. Provided the opportunity to live life on my terms. It has provided the freedom and the wealth to achieve anything I desire.

Today, I'm a multiple income stream coach and mentor covering online businesses, property, digital and precious metal investing. I work with clients in 13 countries. I'm an author of 23 books published in 15 countries and a No 1 Best Selling Author in six countries.

When I became an entrepreneur, little did I realise how many times I would make history – five times, according to the newspaper interviewer, and I'm twice in the Guinness World Records.

I didn't set out to make history, nor to be a Guinness World Record holder, I simply did what I loved doing: being an entrepreneur.

# Karen Newton

Karen is a serial entrepreneur, investor, author and speaker. One day, a guy stopped her in the street asking if she was the author of the book he was holding, and would she coach him? That was the start of Karen Newton International, a global financial education company with clients in 13 countries.

Zero to Millionaire is her signature program which focuses on helping clients develop multiple income streams through creating online businesses; building property portfolios using options; investing in digital products such as shares and cryptocurrencies and protecting the investments with precious metal assets. She is proud of her track record of creating millionaires.

Today, she lives in a Spanish fishing village with her husband and daughter and loves watching sunsets over the bay while enjoying traditional Spanish culture.

Connect with Karen through her biz app, Karen Newton International, available on Google Play Store or Apple.

www.facebook.com/karennewtoninternational

www.instagram.com/newydd105

www.twitter.com/newydd105

INSPIRATIONAL WOMEN OF THE WORLD

# CHAPTER 12:

## Kelly Monroe

---

### Experience is the Best Teacher

What makes an entrepreneur successful is a question that is readily asked by budding entrepreneurs. Is it down to luck, contacts, who you know, hard work, knowledge, energy, drive and a damn good idea?

Well, in part yes to all of the above! But what makes an entrepreneur become successful is experience, learned experience. The old saying 'Experience is the best teacher' is very true and for me in my life at 44 years old I can honestly bear witness to the truth of these words.

Experience doesn't necessarily have to be undergone personally but can be learned through others and our own individual life lessons. Throughout my early years, teens and 20s, I pushed myself to become successful by learning from the example set by my hard-working grandparents and parents. There was no internet, no TED Talks, YouTube or inspirational life coach, there were just books in the library and my own drive to feed a winning mindset.

From the ages of five to 15, all my time was spent working, selling, grafting and being entrepreneurial with my genetic body double, my identical twin.

Reflecting back, I can remember that at the tender age of five the seeds of social entrepreneurialism were sown in me. My mother was called to my primary school by my head teacher; my twin sister and I were being told off and excluded for setting up a protection racket that took money from rich kids to help poor kids to eat school dinners, and in the process took out the school bully twice our age. Back then, social enterprises weren't a thing but in a rather bizarre Robin Hood kind of way this was my first social enterprise. My sense of fairness and equality for all was felt at the age of five and has been maintained even to this day, in my current business dealings working with young people in education. I support young people with free school meals to access learning programmes that are centred around creativity and entrepreneurialism.

When I think about my school life it's ironic; I liked learning but I hated the education system and the archaic rules, a feeling I still hold in part. School for me at times was a battle ground. I hated science, maths and technical subjects as they didn't inspire me, and I poured my attention and time into creative subjects and making things that made money. I had many side hustles in school selling Scotch 3M tape, pens, accessories, all from my desk or rucksack.

Outside of school my twin sister and I had built up a rather extensive window cleaning business, lumping ladders around for miles on end but earning hundreds of pounds each day from the mere outgoings of soap and water. We also used to attend Ministry of Defence auctions, buying up old army gear which we sold on our market stall every weekend. One of the best buys led me to procuring 1,000 old field kitchens stored up and gathering dust since WW2. These heavy lumps of iron weighed a lot and needed two articulated lorries to ship them back to our family farm in Bridgend.

Much to my poor mother's disbelief, 1,000 of these field kitchens were unceremoniously plonked in the field, with my mother crying in despair. But with belief, the gift of the gab, my twin sister and I set about repurposing these old field kitchens into barbecues, dog food kitchens, candle makers' wax pots... amidst a vast array of sales patters that sold every single one, much to everyone's disbelief. We literally were raking it in, so much so that aged 16 we bought our motorcycles, at 17 we bought our cars, and before our 18th birthday I bought my first property from an auction in cash.

When I reflect upon these experiences, it shows that if you have vision and see a gap in the market you can create a product/ service to sell, it's that simple! But I learned early on that to be truly successful you need an education to fall back on. This was something that I had not grasped aged 15 when I nearly threw away my GCSEs but was helped to appreciate and to love learning by an awesome teacher called Mr Edwards, who made me see that my education was important and could open doorways to opportunities.

Aged 15 I invented a device called Parkavan; designed to move a caravan as part of a D&T project, this steered me back towards education as well as entrepreneurship. After entering a UK engineering competition and beating hundreds of brain box kids, I won the category of the Young Engineer for Britain 1994 Awards. This experience spring-boarded me and my twin into a world of rubbing shoulders with entrepreneurs, designers, scientists and researchers, and created in me a desire to help women get into these subjects, something unheard of in the early 90s. I was featured on Tomorrow's World, travelled to parts of Europe, and was part of research projects, all before my 16th birthday.

This experience opened my eyes to bigger business and how infrastructures were essential for success, and led me to be invited to work on a project getting women and girls into these industries, called WISE – Women Into Science and Engineering. This project was supported by the University of Glamorgan and led to many future government-funded spin-off schemes in STEM, the educational integration of science, technology, engineering, and mathematics, helping thousands of women and girls access skills, education and connections to get them into these industries. I even met the Queen as part of an organised event to garner support for this amazing cause. Not a bad outcome for a kid who never passed her maths or science GCSEs and was told by some teachers that she wouldn't amount to much.

Experience is indeed the greatest teacher but it was a great teacher who made me love learning again, and despite my struggles with academia I learned to love education and successfully, with my trusted twin sister, worked and ran various business ventures whilst balancing studying for A levels, and then passed with a 2:1 Honours degree from Cardiff University.

Life after university became very interesting when I landed a job as the City Editor for a publication company backed by the up and coming celebrity chef Jamie Oliver. This led me to learn how to build teams, sell concepts, create, write and edit copy, convince investors to part with large sums of money and negotiate distribution deals with big chain retailers like John Menzies, Borders and Virgin. I was even involved in developing the early form of online media which we now know as smartphone technology, but back then it was called Wireless Application Protocol or WAP.

After a few heady years travelling the UK and doing insane things, I decided it was time to come nearer to home, said goodbye to the Editor's role and landed a seemingly reserved job as a Business

Development Manager working for a company specialising in technology, training and development. After a few years working as an intrapreneur, I took the plunge back to being an entrepreneur.

Armed with £10k in savings, a ton of experience, an education and bundles of energy, I set about building a business that was keen to support young people and businesses with innovative educational and entrepreneurialism services that inspire aspirations and change.

Fast forward to today, 21 years on, and I can honestly say the journey to running, managing and leading a successful business has been far from easy. There have been moments of joy and fist-pumping achievements right through to adversity, disappointments, losses and lessons in life that have taught me about other people and, most importantly, myself. It has been a daily learning curve, investing in and building up a successful business that has vision, infrastructure and a skilled team. It all sounds easy, but it takes time, effort and massive commitment.

Working as an entrepreneur and a female businesswoman is tough. Education, the school of life and knocks are key to building resilience and knowledge. Everything happens for a reason, and if the Universe has taught me one thing, when you get a no, it's generally telling you for a damn good reason. If you want to be taken seriously you have to be serious about yourself. You cannot create depth if there isn't substance and education is everything, no one stops learning.

My advice to anyone working for a business, or for those thinking of setting up a business or growing a business, is to start with the basics or go back to basics, value learning, educate yourself and surround yourself with people thirsty for knowledge.

Indeed, experience is the best teacher – but you never forget a great teacher!

# Kelly Monroe

Kelly Monroe is an innovative business coach, inspirational trainer and public speaker running a successful multi-sited SME Welsh business, Really Pro Ltd.

After senior leadership roles Kelly achieved numerous awards and accolades for innovation, engineering, marketing and business management. She believes lifelong learning and skilled people are the backbone of successful businesses and resilient communities.

Kelly pours passion and energy into working within Welsh educational and business sectors. As cofounder of innovative EdTech Software company Together Platforms Ltd, she helps young people and businesses reach their full potential through the development and delivery of innovative learning programmes and use of emerging software technologies.

After several life-altering events, Kelly came back from adversity and is the embodiment of never giving up. Believing in paying it forward, any of her spare time is spent volunteering and helping others through community outreach work, whilst managing three naughty sausage dogs at home.

kelly@reallypro.co.uk

www.linkedin.com/in/kelly-monroe-b22ba97b

INSPIRATIONAL WOMEN OF THE WORLD

# CHAPTER 13:

## Leanne Naylor

---

**Sleep and why putting a plaster on the wound isn't always the best medicine**

I believe sleep underpins our entire wellbeing – emotional, mental, and physical – health is wealth.

I'm a firm believer that sleep, and not just any sleep, underpins our entire wellbeing including our emotional, mental, spiritual and physical health – after all, health is our wealth.

I know this because of both my professional and lived experience, in which I have supported people throughout my years in the NHS and in private practice who have struggled with their sleep for decades. Struggling to sleep, stay asleep and never feeling refreshed and energised despite having tried all the lotions and potions, physiological test results showing as negative, so they all just carried on as usual, not knowing what caused it, until they hit crisis point.

This crisis point I really resonate with, having struggled with sleeplessness at various times in my life, and by that I mean *really* struggled to sleep, averaging only two hours a night at best and in chunks of maybe 15–30 minutes at a time. This went on for *months*.

During this period, I would go through phases of feeling OK, sometimes feeling quite energetic and even making it to the gym. Other times, I would literally feel *so* exhausted physically and emotionally, struggling to sleep, waking numerous times per night, I could barely get myself dressed and into work, just dragging myself through each day.

This went on for several months, to the point where I knew I couldn't carry on and was at risk of complete burnout. Having worked in mental health for over 15 years, I have seen first-hand what severe sleep deprivation can do (a weakened immune system and mental health problems such as anxiety and depression) which ultimately can lead to devastating effects.

Sleep is a primary need for all humans; it is as important as eating, drinking and breathing and it is also the only time our bodies (physically and mentally) are given time to rest simultaneously.

So, off I trotted to the GP… It didn't go well, I cried like an absolute baby – imagine the scene…. Floods of tears, snotty, red faced and unable to tell him what the problem was. Eventually, I mumbled some words about not sleeping and told him exactly what was going on. What I didn't expect was the look on his face, one of sheer horror and silence. He then advised me how lucky I was to not have become psychotic… WTF? I was like, as if 'I' would ever become psychotic.

I was given prescriptions for antidepressants and sleeping tablets, neither of which I wanted and neither of which I took. I told him this and asked for alternative support, instead of which he advised there wasn't anything else.

So off I went, feeling totally lost. Thinking WTF do I do now...? Sat in the car and cried relentlessly for about an hour. Not a pretty sight. I pulled myself together and went for a walk, which was peaceful and serene. It allowed me to think, without all the other noise of life distracting me about what I needed to do, to get myself back on track and sleeping properly again.

A few things I made non-negotiable: investing in a therapist, having a good sleep and daytime routine, and making sure I was getting outside and working on my mindset for at least 20 minutes each day respectively.

I know sleep is unique to the individual; I also know that sleep is innate, and we can use the power of our mind to improve our sleep.

You see, a good quality sleep is unique to the individual. What isn't different for each person is that sleep is innate (except for around 3% of the population). We are born to sleep, so if we are not sleeping and there is not a psychological health reason precipitating the sleeplessness, then it is likely to be linked to your mindset, on both a conscious and subconscious level.

Insomnia or sleeplessness is usually based upon a fear, anxiety or stress activating an alert state, which is essentially activating our autonomic nervous system making us feel very awake and 'on edge' aka adrenaline.

When this happens, a deep unbroken sleep is going to be difficult for you to achieve because your subconscious mind is telling you 'I could be in danger, I need to be alert,' so it automatically prevents you from sleeping as a defence mechanism, to 'protect you'.

This is what happened with me; I had 1,000 'tabs' open in my mind, ruminating on all sorts of things, whilst other nights, absolutely *nothing* with no idea why I was lying there awake – again.

This would happen, it would come and go over a period because I did 'all the things', all the 'external things': a couple of drinks before bed, keeping busy (super busy and working crazy hours – which worked well for my career, but not advisable), going out with friends. Basically, anything and everything to 'keep myself busy and hopefully tire me out'.

But… the sleepless nights would always creep back in every now and then, sometimes for months at a time. Each time, I would try a 'new thing' a new type of yoga, meditation, more exercise and even sleeping tablets at one point. All of which were somewhat useful, but none of which got to the root cause and hence, I struggled to resolve it once and for all because I was simply just putting a 'plaster on the wound'.

Thing is, all the above can be helpful to a degree and even resolve sleeplessness temporarily, but for it to be a lasting resolve you need to remove any limiting beliefs and teach your subconscious that is it OK to sleep. If you've tried all the 'lotions, potions and gadgets' to no avail and physiologically there isn't anything causing your sleeplessness, I really encourage you not to let it get to crisis point, as so many of my clients (myself included) have done, allowing months, years and even decades to pass by on minimal sleep. They knew something needed to change but they felt stuck, just like I did. They needed help to become 'unstuck' and know the why and the how, because you can't change something you don't understand.

You can RESOLVE your poor sleep easily and effortlessly, without medication and with 100% commitment.

The first thing to understand is: sleep is innate and it's OK to re-learn what you were born with and unlearn the sleeplessness habit that in some way thinks it has been protecting you – because it really is not. You see, knowing you can unlearn the sleeplessness habit and reinstall what we were born with is the first step to resolving your sleep easily and effortlessly for lasting resolve.

Second is knowing, and admitting, you're stuck. So many of my clients from friends, colleagues and various corporate and entrepreneurial backgrounds all came to me at crisis point because they were stuck and didn't know what else to do. Almost all of them struggled with deep-rooted negative beliefs about themselves, some of which they weren't consciously aware of, which is exactly why I combine conscious and subconscious therapeutic work for rapid, lasting change.

There is also the need to be motivated and committed, because one key element of any change or success story is you must be 100% committed to engaging in the work, doing the work (both internal and external) and wanting the change.

It is this internal change that I have noticed brings the most profound changes, because the truth is to *resolve* our sleep and not just put a plaster on the wound. We need to do the inner work, accessing our conscious and subconscious mind to get to the root cause and seek resolve for good.

We can all resolve our sleep, no matter how old we are or how long the issues have been present, but we need the commitment, motivation and desire for change to fuel us to dig deep into our core belief system – the answer often lies within.

Commitment isn't 'trying' as this implies failure. Take action, go all in with full focus and commitment to yourself, because you are your best supporter.

This is what I help my clients with – the internal and external, by helping them to understand and get to the root cause (often the deep-rooted core beliefs), re-wire the negatives to positives, using a combination of therapy, science and energy work. This unique combination enables my clients to resolve their sleep issues without years of therapy or medication, allowing them the freedom to be in control of their sleep and their life.

Just don't put a plaster on the wound, because it might be a quick fix but it will not give you the lasting resolve you crave.

Sleep and mindset are my passion and it's OK to ask for help and reach out.

## Leanne Naylor

Leanne is an award-winning clinical lead within the NHS, a therapist, hypnotherapist and sleep consultant, with over 15 years' experience of working within mental health supporting both adults and children.

She has seen first-hand how sleep is a key component to our mental wellbeing and overall functioning, through both her work within various mental health services and her own lived experience in which her own sleep issues once greatly impacted her life.

Leanne is passionate about sleep and helping others to resolve their sleep issues, often presenting to numerous different professionals. She can also be found as guest speaker on podcasts, talking about all things sleep and helping professionals and entrepreneurs overcome their sleep issues without the need for medication or years of therapy.

Leanne currently resides in the county of Kent, UK, with her partner and enjoys time out in the countryside walking with her pug.

www.leannenaylor.com

www.facebook.com/LNRapidtransformationalcoach

www.instagram.com/leanne_thesleepconsultant

# CHAPTER 14:

## Michelle Wyngaard

Living life in alignment with your values and top five passions leads to your ultimate success and happiness

### The journey of self-discovery

Life is energy. Energy cannot be lost but transferred. I now realise we come into this world with the blueprint of what we need to fulfil our purpose in life. Our life's journey is to go through adversity, however painful, to teach us a series of lessons to prepare us, if we are ready and willing, to follow the path of transformation.

You are blessed with divine gifts if you choose to go through this challenge and then teach others the lesson or accept what is and repeat cycles. Do you ever catch yourself saying, 'Why does this always happen to me?' The aim is to awaken from our sleep state as human beings; we have free will and the choice to do what we want. Balancing the two is the challenge. It is our blessing and burden. Happiness is an inside job; we tend to seek it externally, moving further from the source of energy and wonder why we feel more unfulfilled or temporarily satisfied. Learn the 12 Laws of the Universe to guide you through life. It will be enlightening.

Strive towards achieving your highest vibration, living life in joy and bliss. Don't get triggered by the small stuff that satisfies the ego. It is a waste of energy. Eckhart Tolle wrote *The Power of Now* – this present moment is all we have; cherish it. Time is our only currency, the money we can always make again. Our conditioned mind blocks us from breaking through the limitations imposed on us from childhood or adult trauma bonds. We self-sabotage for not being good enough, or self-worth issues based on material measures that are soul-destroying.

An awakened soul learns not to become triggered by the material worth as they know their true spiritual nature. The emotional memory remains etched in our mind as if it is still experiencing the same scenario despite its past trauma. The mind cannot distinguish the difference and releases the same chemicals. We give our power away to the mind through the habit of our conditioning until we can't determine what the heart wants. I believe that human beings tend to subconsciously hold on to their suffering as we become accustomed to it and don't know how to forgive ourselves and others. Let go – it is past the expiry date. We tend to ruminate the death out of old feelings, causing unnecessary suffering.

We can use this energy to focus on our personal growth. Hire a coach or mentor to guide you. The mind is lazy and chooses to replay what is easy instead of forming new pathways of development. It gets stuck in the cycle resulting in repeated self-sabotaging habits. I was very privileged to have met Michael Gerber in London. The key takeaway question from that meeting was 'What is missing in your business?' – *you* – work *on* your business, not *in* your business.

## Know your values and passions as your compass for your goals

Plan how and where and with whom you want to invest your time and energy. One of my most respected coaches, Dr John Demartini, teaches how to determine your values and impact your goals. The assessment tool is free on his website.

To be more productive, use energy batching instead of time management. Review your values every six months.

As a certified passion test facilitator, I help you find your top five passions in life if you feel stuck. Your passions are like the breadcrumbs leading to your goals. Our mission and purpose are to inspire transformation through love in service to all humanity.

This passion test is the brainchild of Janet Attwood who says if faced with a decision, challenge or opportunity, always choose in favour of your top five passions. This process helped me break through to select the direction of my life's purpose consciously.

Plan how your business goals can support your personal goals to align with your living vision for when your life is ideal by future projecting.

Practise self-mastery in one area that you are truly passionate about until you can monetise on it. Place any shiny object ideas until you monetise in one area as pending. What you resist will persist, work on your strong areas and the weak areas that block your progression.

The Law of the Universe will always have the opposite of what we are seeking. Be grateful for both lessons.

You are the one holding you back from living your best life for what you came here for – to dance the dance of life until the end and say it was a great life.

Your battles will leave scars; however, you will be stronger for having faced them.

Your words have power knowing this, be intentional about what you want from life. Go and live your life and get out of your way and live an unstoppable life to do whatever you want to do.

Be willing to do whatever it takes to break through, gain clarity and creative focus, be decisive to go full throttle and release the brakes on living life full out.

Trust the voice inside your heart; never let the mind control your destiny. Don't let your past define you, but let it refine you. I once met a billionaire, Errol Abrahams. He told me if your why is not big enough and does not make you cry, get a bigger *why* – profound. You have got to want to jump out of bed to do it without being asked to action.

"Unless you truly understand what you value most, what truly inspires you most, who you truly are, and your true purpose, a completely inspired, fulfilling life will elude you." – Dr John Demartini.

As a seasoned entrepreneur, the important thing is how quickly you get up and carry on.

## Invest in yourself continuously

Find a reputable coach or mentor who resonates with you, and you will need to upgrade them in alignment with your growth. Trust your gut in this – choose one who tells you what you need to hear, not what you want to hear. Remember to be open and coachable to learn and recondition your mind to remove blocks from childhood and negative money beliefs that no longer serve you. Be conscious of your limiting belief systems and replace them with unlimited thoughts. Be bold and fearless despite the odds. Life is happening for you, not to you. My first business coach taught me to stop listening to GOOP – the good opinion of other people.

Remember, you are your best asset; therefore, sacrifice to invest more in you. Don't overthink the investment in yourself because you are projecting your conditioned beliefs about "I can't afford to." Instead, ask "How can I afford it?" Then your brain starts activating, and finds ways of how you can make it happen. The first autobiography that inspired me was Sir Richard Branson's – 'If faced with an opportunity in life, say yes now and the how will figure itself out.' We get stuck on the how, instead focus on the what and the why.

Celebrate your micro wins. Females are generally not good at praising themselves, myself included. Master learning to love yourself unconditionally and practise self-care. Women are natural nurturers. Please put on your oxygen mask first and learn to say no when you mean no to allow you to focus on your goals one at a time until you master it as the authority.

You will be hit by the shiny object syndromes as you develop, trust me, the mind fools you to distract you from what is uncomfortable to slow you from your progress. Today our biggest challenge is distraction avoidance. Our minds are wired to move away from pain/discomfort and towards pleasure/comfort. The truth is that as you fledge into entrepreneurship, you want to do everything at once, leading to FOMO syndrome (fear of missing out). Would you mind placing those ideas on the back burner? Or risk the dilution of your top goals and drivers for success? Watch out for the success thief which creeps up on you – procrastination and imposter syndrome, our modern-day fear of success avoidance.

"You can't spell challenge without change." – Courtney Blunlove

"How you show up is how you perform; be present in how you want to see yourself in the future." – Dr John Demartini

Focus on your personal growth and grow your network which is your net worth. Join like-minded groups online and ask for help if you need help. Don't give up on the first few hurdles. It is just part of the journey which makes you more resilient. Learn the art of how to communicate, speak and negotiate skills, get to know your KPI numbers, build a trustworthy team around you and have a close circle of confidants you can rely on for emotional support.

# Michelle Wyngaard

Michelle Wyngaard, a forward-thinking dentist from Cape Town, is the proprietor of Dynamic Dental Studio in England. Despite challenging apartheid times, she graduated in 1997. After a year of practising, she emigrated from South Africa to join NHS services for three years, then joined a private practice.

Her purpose and vision is to transform a million smiles in her lifetime. She believes that creating a healthy and beautiful smile can be life-changing. She states, "Your smile is the first and last thing people remember you by, therefore investing in it wisely will pay dividends in your life in the long term."

She followed her true calling in 2016 despite the fear of drifting from the comfort of her dentistry career. Instead, Michelle embarked on a personal development journey, discovering her true passions and values for what she wanted to be, have and do to lead herself to fulfilment and success in life.

www.linkedin.com/in/dentalpreneurcoach

INSPIRATIONAL WOMEN OF THE WORLD

# CHAPTER 15:

## Naomi Holbrook

---

### Unbecoming

"Maybe the journey isn't so much about *becoming* anything. Maybe it's about *unbecoming* everything that isn't really you so you can become who you were always meant to be."

The past six years has been the ultimate journey of self-discovery, development and self-empowerment and ultimately unlearning a lot of what and *who* I thought I was.

Before I carry on I feel it's important to share a little context.

Since as early as I can remember I battled with different areas of my life.

School was a particularly stressful and difficult time for me. I attended a private girls' school, which had an excellent reputation for turning out high achievers. However, I was not one of them and felt I had to work extraordinarily hard just to scrape through in most subjects.

During my adolescent years I had regular periods of absence from school for different health reasons, resulting in me spending my weekends and school holidays catching up on coursework and receiving additional private tutoring my parents funded just to enable me to advance to the next academic year.

Not long after I started secondary school my mum became seriously ill. She was forced to leave her nursing career due to her rapidly declining health. This had a disruptive effect on our family and home life, which further impacted on my ability to concentrate on schoolwork and had a significant and prolific effect on my mental health, which I wouldn't appreciate the effect of for many years to come.

I battled with anxiety, depression and very low self-esteem which did nothing for my lack in confidence and fuelled the lack of belief I had in my ability to succeed at most things.

I left school in 1991 with a few very low-grade GCSEs and was fairly adamant the last thing I wanted to do was anything highly academic, so I enrolled in a Cosmetology & Hairdressing course at my local technical college in the hope that I would be able to make a living afterwards.

I didn't have very high expectations for myself.

Despite the traumatic loss of my mum in the summer of 1994, I attended my final year of college and qualified in Cosmetology, Anatomy, Physiology and Massage and was fairly astounded when I was offered a position at one of the UK's premier health spa resorts.

It was here that I made the decision to go to university, and studied part time whilst working. I graduated in Business Studies with a

Distinction, enabling me to redirect my career in a managerial direction.

My career continued to excel from there, which surprised no one more than me. I worked hard in every position and climbed the career ladder with some of the most prestigious and luxury brands in the world, yet I still lacked a true belief in myself and often thought I would be caught out and let go from various positions for not having the required level of qualifications, something now referred to as 'imposter syndrome' and which, whilst you are reading this, you may also have suffered.

## You don't have to be ready to change, you just have to want to

In 2014, unaware at the time, I started my full transformation of *unbecoming.*

It's a deep misconception that you believe you need to be ready to make big changes in your life; mostly you just need to be in enough discomfort to no longer want to stay where you are. It's rarely anything to do with being ready and more about a deep sense of fear of failure, or in some cases success, that keeps us where we are. We don't truly believe that we can accomplish the things we truly want, or in my case I didn't believe that I deserved them. I was in a lot of discomfort, both physically and mentally.

For the best part of my adult life I had used food and alcohol to comfort myself through traumatic and stressful periods in my life. I had bounced from diet to diet, always looking for the quickest fix for a holiday, an event, or a quick boost of confidence, but nothing I ever did was sustainable. I gained weight and lost weight and each time my self-confidence skyrocketed and plummeted too.

I was at the time 39 years old and from the outside looking in it probably looked like I had my life pretty much together. I was independent with a 'successful' 20+ year career in the Wellbeing & Beauty industry.

Yet away from the outside world I felt far from together, or successful. I had thrown myself into my career for over 20 years. Always feeling like I was catching up from school, trying to prove myself and putting more and more pressure on myself to succeed; working longer hours, later nights, commuting for 16 of the years and neglecting my physical and mental health for a vast majority of the time.

Once I finally had enough I started to make daily improvements to my health, eliminating the alcohol from my diet, starting to pay attention to what I was eating and taking regular exercise, which most of the time meant a 5am run before getting the 7am train for my daily commute to London!

For years I had been telling myself I didn't have the time to exercise, I deserved the take-aways at the weekend and the glasses of wine every night after work, but they were just the excuses I repeated to myself to make me feel better about the lack of action I was taking to change my situation.

Towards the end of 2015 it was clear to me that I was on the brink of burnout. I was ashamed to admit it to myself, let alone anyone else, and I no longer felt the passion for my career or the way I was living that I once had. I had spent 20+ years building my career and the thought of walking out and leaving it filled me with dread, but I did the unthinkable and in 2016, shortly before turning 41, I left corporate life.

## Self-belief and resilience

I now believe my purpose has always been driven towards helping others, to want to see them achieve their true potential when they didn't always believe they could. Maybe there is a little irony there that I would look for it in others before I could find it in myself. When I changed my life through my own health transformation I knew I wanted to share that passion and empower other women to do the same too.

I returned to studying in 2017 and qualified as a Nutrition & Weight Management Coach, then launched my own Online Coaching business, Wellthy Evolution®.

Leaving 20+ years in the corporate world behind and starting my own business was quite honestly terrifying and full of valuable lessons. I went from having support functions accessible all around me to doing everything myself, but one of the strengths I believe I have developed over the years, not just in my professional life but also in my personal one, is tenacity. If I don't know it, I'll learn it despite how long it takes me!

It's only in the last few years I have come to realise how much I held myself back based on the limitations I had put upon myself and it is something I see so frequently in the women I coach and the many women I meet.

We think we are going to fail before we have even tried, when in fact our biggest failing is never trying in the first place. My own health transformation, and my clients', has taught me that you have to build momentum.

You don't get healthy by eating one nutritiously balanced meal just like you don't get successful overnight in business. People rarely see the small, repetitive actions you take on a daily basis to achieve your ultimate goals, but whether it be in your health journey or in your business, *consistency* can be the difference between success and failure.

The journey is rarely linear, very few are, and through having my own business and through the challenges I have overcome in my personal life I've discovered that it is often necessary to change the route multiple times, but you must *never* give up on your goal!

If there is one message I wish you to take away from this chapter it is to become your own cheerleader, to *believe* that you have the ability in life to achieve whatever you desire. Whether it be to lose the weight you have battled with and live a healthier, happier and longer life, or to start your own business and live the life you create with passion and purpose – stop limiting yourself based on a story you have told yourself for so long that you have come to accept it as true.

I'm not going to say it will be easy every day, I still have moments of self-doubt when I am not sure I can achieve my biggest goals, but here's something a lot of people may not wish to tell you – we all do.

# Naomi Holbrook

Naomi is a certified Nutrition, Weightloss & Transformation Coach and creator of Educate. Empower. Evolve by Wellthy Evolution®. She empowers busy professional women to put an end to yo-yo dieting and create optimal health whilst releasing weight and rebalancing their hormones through her signature online group and VIP coaching programmes.

Naomi qualified in Cosmetology, Anatomy, Physiology and Massage in 1995, starting her career as a beauty therapist in health spa resorts and luxury five-star hotels across the UK. For the last 11 years of her 20+ year career, Naomi was responsible for sales across the UK and Ireland for several divisions of luxury skincare and cosmetic brands.

Naomi grew up in a small market town in North Devon. She now lives in Hove where she again embraces coastal life with open water swimming, paddle boarding and regularly exploring the beautiful Sussex countryside. She dreams of having her own dog one day.

www.facebook.com/naomi.holbrook

www.instagram.com/naomi_holbrook_coach

www.linkedin.com/in/naomi-holbrook-14188737

# CHAPTER 16:

## Nicky Bright

---

**You only need a few pounds to start a business and turn it into a million-pound business**

My world, my only world came tumbling down. I lost everything in life, the only life I had built and known. I lost my family, home, job, two little dogs and finally my car. Approaching 50 years of age, there was no way that I would have the years ahead of me to start all over again and build what I had lost.

How wrong I was; this was my first mistake, a negative thought, belief.

People say you need money to create money. Don't doubt your dreams, doubt will stop you achieving.

I received my last employed pay cheque not knowing how I was going to meet the following month's mortgage, bills, even food. I remember thinking: I have to do something, it's just me and the children now. I had to find a way to survive. The bills kept arriving, how could I stop them arriving? One after the other, every day scared to come down the stairs to see mail on the hall floor.

Changing habits, teaching the children how to change the way we had always lived, that was the hardest part. Lights left on, heating full blast, fridge always empty, I was on a losing battle and the bills kept arriving, with no income. What I've learned is *fear won't pay your bills* – when you focus on the fear of receiving those dreaded letters they keep arriving. When it's the only focus on your mind, it becomes the only subject you think about. Changing my focus was how I stopped the letters arriving.

The smell of fear, maybe it is a true saying, maybe you can smell it?

I was just a few days old when the doctors told my parents nothing would save me and to prepare for end of life. My father, then only 19 years old, tells me how he placed me inside his T-shirt and wouldn't go to sleep as he feared he would lose me during the night. Just a few days old and the smell of fear was around me. Tiny, I stayed inside my father's T-shirt clinging on to life with him keeping me warm. He talked to me all night telling me he loved me and how important I was to him. You have to fight now, be strong he whispered to me.

Jumping ahead nine years later, the lady I loved and looked up to, my grandmother, passed away in my bedroom, in my bed. I remember being very scared. I closed my eyes as I entered the room and ran back out. I wanted to say goodbye and give her a kiss, but I was scared, scared of the dark and death.

I said I would never sleep in that bedroom again or the bed my grandmother had passed away in. I was scared to even open the bedroom door. I remember praying, asking to never be scared again. My mother told me to stay in her bedroom and not to look out of the window as the ambulance was arriving to take Nanny. I heard a van outside, doors opening and closing and voices talking. I climbed onto my mother's dressing table and peeked through a gap in the curtains. I saw them carrying my grandmother out in a black body bag. My mother screaming as they carried her mother out; she was on her knees with my father wrapped around her.

Forty years later fear returned and this time it brought me to my knees… I thought I had mastered fear, but it returns and shows up when you least expect it!

I found myself lying in the dark on the sofa crying, sobbing, questioning what went wrong? Spinning in my mind was my life, the day I met my husband, our first home, birth of children, holidays and memories, total torment. Twenty-five years married to a person I thought I knew better than myself left me broken. How was I going to figure out a plan after my life had just hit reset?

I was having a normal busy day in store, managing staff along with daily trading business. I remember the day well, the store was busy and the telephone kept ringing and ringing, I remember looking around and all staff were engaged serving customers. The incoming call was on redial, I looked over to see a cashier become available. I heard her greeting the caller… "She's busy at the moment, can I take a message?" I turned and made eye contact with the cashier, and she informed me, "It's an urgent call."

I felt something was wrong, a feeling, an intuition you can only explain for a split second; your surroundings feel different as if you are looking at yourself as a different, person in slow motion.

I took the call. It was my son, and I asked if it could wait until I arrived home. He was agitated, breathing fast and upset. My first thought was: his dad had an accident. The store was full of people,

I stood beside the cash till and listened to what my son was about to tell me.

What I was to discover from that phone call was about to change my life, not just my life but all of our lives, forever. The news was about to bring me to my knees with the biggest fall I have ever taken... "Mum, Dad's having an affair."

I remember standing in the middle of the store on the telephone questioning the news I had just received. I was left standing frozen in time. I looked around and everyone around me was laughing, joking, smiling, serving customers. I felt I wasn't inside my own body, a sense of free falling. I remember thinking I had to go home; without even considering anything else I collected my coat, bag, car keys and left for home.

I lived a short distance from the store, just a 10-minute journey; what was I about to discover?

What was to happen over the coming months was a 'reset' of my life... I lost not only my husband, but family, pets, car, home, and finally my job!

Only I could save my self, home and children. I used all my skills from my careers and started to create a business plan. With less than 99p in the bank, I started my business with nothing except my four walls, turning my home into my business, Holiday Home Agency. I was really excited and full of ideas.

I learned about a government funding programme to educate yourself with new skills and straight away signed up. I looked into further government schemes – Business Enterprise – so much help and support including grants to help set you up in business, being self-employed, taking your dream forward.

Once I was given the information I was excited, I took up on my inspirational thoughts and ideas and started a business plan.

How do you start a business when you have no income and no money left in the bank? Think of yourself as a refugee who leaves their country with only the clothes they wear and everything they once owned is left behind. 'Fight or flight' – what would you do? What strengths do you have? What do you believe you're good at? Focus only on your four walls, and what you can control. Start researching, educating yourself. Knowledge will give you confidence, belief that you can offer a service better than your competitors.

How did I get this far? If I stayed where I was out of work I wouldn't be where I wanted to be, I had to evolve! Fear is the biggest hold-back that will stop you achieving. I had a background of interior styling, estate agency and retail management. I knew my strengths within each role as well as my passion.

I started with nothing, I knew once I received my first booking I would use that income to grow my business.

I did everything on my own, I was the cleaner, gardener, window cleaner, accountant, IT, marketing and business networker. I kept different shoes in the boot of my car from entrepreneur business woman to painter and decorator. Every evening I sat for hours studying, creating and looking for new business. Once I put all my skills together I was excited and knew my focus and actions would lead to my future goal and result.

Just three weeks in and the news of Covid closed me down and fear returned once again, except this time I knew what I needed to do: focus and come up with a plan. During this difficult year I focused only on keeping fear out of my life because when you do, only a positive outcome happens.

Fear is the unknown, something that hasn't happened or doesn't even exist!

I'm now currently creating a second business supplying the furnishings for holiday homes. From 99p and being made homeless, I now have a business heading for its first million.

# Nicky Bright

Nicky Bright is known for her originality and sheer determination forged with self-belief. But her journey would have indicated many other paths. A highly successful holiday home expert and stylist, she started as a polished professional in the corporate world with many years' experience in project management and business sourcing. However, everything Nicky had worked for over 25 years was threatened; she was faced with tough decisions, a point of no return.

Nicky has courage with a crystal-clear plan for her future. She has a determination to follow her dreams no matter what life throws at her, and the focus to unearth her creative vision so it can benefit others in the pursuit of their own creative journey.

Nicky now has two thriving businesses after overcoming crushing adversity. She is a woman with depth, who will never steer from her path of purpose in life.

www.nickybrightholidays.com

www.nickybright.com

www.Instagram.com/nickybrightholidays

INSPIRATIONAL WOMEN OF THE WORLD

# CHAPTER 17:

## Stacey Cann

---

### My Secret to Success: Adversity

Strength comes from your darkest moments.

I believe it is no coincidence that many women who overcome adversity go on to be successful entrepreneurs, in much the same way that innovation often comes from necessity. Take for example the invention of the lightbulb, which came about during the Great Depression of the 1930s.

My own experience with adversity is, in fact, the secret to my business success. Surviving the darkest times in my life instilled in me a determination that now drives me in entrepreneurship.

It took some major life events to make me re-evaluate how I wanted to spend my work life. In my shining corporate career of more than 10 years, I'd been overlooked for promotion while on maternity leave and made to feel ashamed of my mental health struggles, including anxiety. This string of events shattered my confidence.

Without those dark times, I'd almost certainly still be working my way through my corporate career without any thought of being my own boss. Having been treated so badly, I'd lost my love of the corporate world and I knew I wanted to succeed at being self-employed. I made the decision to buy a franchise business that gave me new skills and utilised my existing marketing and business experience. My health improved and the paediatric first aid business was a success. I bought additional territories to continue growing.

I didn't know it, but my darkest moments were still yet to come. A few years later, after a complicated twin pregnancy, one of my babies needed lifesaving surgery at just five weeks old. He and I spent four months in a paediatric intensive care unit, 20 miles away from his twin brother, dad and three-year-old sister.

The trauma was extreme but I pushed myself to continue running my paediatric first aid franchise from his hospital bedside as a coping mechanism to keep me occupied. The situation was immensely tough, but I was not prepared for the 12 months that followed after he eventually left hospital. Not only was I living with inflammatory bowel disease, I was struggling with depression and anxiety, bringing up three small children and also trying to run a business.

On the days I wanted to hide or run away, I couldn't. My family needed me and I had to put them first. I dug deep, remained resilient and kept going.

Without that experience, I'd have no idea just how capable I am as an entrepreneur. My health struggles as a parent and business owner forced transformation in both me and my business. The frustration at the lack of help for my mental health inspired me to create something I felt was truly needed to help other parents.

It was then that the concept of my second business, Parenting In Mind, became my very own lightbulb moment.

I'm not alone. No businesswoman I've ever spoken to who has experienced such adversity and trauma would have chosen that path for themselves. Yet rather than apologising for their struggle, they have gone on to become successful entrepreneurs.

## You can have illnesses and still be successful: My three steps for success

During my corporate career, I felt embarrassed and impeded by my bowel condition. There were no physical symptoms for people to see, just pain and fatigue for me to manage. Combining that with parenting, at times I'd be so fatigued that all I could do was lie on the sofa.

Those around me would say things like 'Don't put so much pressure on yourself' and 'You need to take it easy'. However, when I listened to those well-intended words, I'd end up feeling worse about myself, leaving me with a lower mood and even less physical energy. It all took its toll on my mental health and I'd question if I was really capable of any of the things I wanted to do.

**Step one** was to accept the situation for what it was and use both my physical and mental health conditions as my source of enablement rather than treating them like a negative imposition. I was a mum who, like many other parents, had experienced a *really* tough time. Life hadn't been ideal, but I now had the perspective to be grateful for what it was rather than wishing for change.

I accepted my own limitations and figured out how to work *with* them. I changed my business model so that my business worked better for me. Then I aligned my expectations around my young family's needs.

**Step two** was to understand and trust myself. Our internal voice is the one that we subconsciously listen to all the time. It is the most important one we hear and we instinctively act on what it tells us. I took the time to learn about how, as human beings, we concoct false narratives to protect ourselves when our brain perceives a threat. I learned about how inhibitions surface as the brain tries to keep us safe.

I went on a mental journey to find self-belief and build back my confidence. I surrounded myself with like-minded people and external influences. This gave me a wonderful realisation that we all have mental health and we all have 'baggage' but it's how we respond to those trials that ultimately makes the difference for a successful entrepreneur.

**Step three** was to redefine what success meant to me. For the first few years of being self-employed, I had institutionalised corporate ideas of what success looked and felt like. Redefining this for me as both a business owner and a parent was a complete game changer.

It released pressure and expectations I had on myself that I didn't even know existed.

## Being honest with yourself to grow

I discovered that I held a lot of mental blocks and limiting beliefs about how people viewed me. I had a clear vision but I felt like a complete imposter – partly because my confidence was low and partly because I didn't yet feel like an expert in helping people with mental health and wellbeing.

I started to push out of my comfort zone and was amazed at what happened as a result. When I let go of my limiting beliefs, I started to thrive. I even won national business awards for being inspirational to others – something I never imagined possible.

In my journey to find self-belief and rebuild my confidence, I discovered the power of my positive mindset, embraced the trauma of past events, let go of my previous self-perception *and* gained new qualifications.

Each time I pushed through a blockage, I felt my subconscious trying to protect me, but reminded myself that these thoughts weren't real. The reward each time wasn't always the outcome I wanted, but I always got a boost in confidence and a reminder that I am resilient. I realised that adversity develops resilience. It has taken me huge resilience to fight through my hardest times and carry on.

Resilience is the key attribute of those that struggle and overcome adversity of any kind.

Running a business needs a high level of resilience. Dealing with adverse situations gave me the core belief that I could get through anything, even a tricky business situation. If, like me, you run businesses where your customers depend on you for life skills, your resilience is part of what they buy into. On the days that you want to quit, when you are scared, when you feel burnt out, you still have to show up. So be honest with yourself and push through anyway. If you don't, you don't have a business because nobody will do it for you.

## Creating your own success

Without realising, our sense of identity is often based on the perception of those around us. We base so much on what we think others see and feel about us. The truth is, however, that our identity is constantly evolving. Be prepared to let go of what others think. Don't let other people's truths become yours. Trust in yourself and be prepared to test your resilience. To let go of ideals and be comfortable with who we are *now* is empowering and uplifting.

Remember, both positive and negative experiences shape us. In business, these experiences can add value, encourage compassion and give you an amazing sense of achievement.

Without going through the worst times in your life, you wouldn't have the same perspective. You would have no idea how resilient you are. You may not have had the courage to push through your fears and succeed.

Next time you think you can't because… remember that you can. Not despite the thing that other people (and you) assume will hold you back but *because* of it.

Success for me has become helping others and making myself feel good. Whilst I wouldn't have chosen to go through such trauma or adversity, I am grateful for the adverse experiences that have shaped my resilience. They are the secret of my success.

## Stacey Cann

Stacey Cann is an award-winning entrepreneur, speaker, coach and mental health advocate.

Before children, Stacey enjoyed corporate success, working with Premiership football clubs and multinational corporations. Since motherhood, she has reshaped her career and now helps new and expecting parents.

Parenting In Mind was inspired by Stacey's own experiences of mental health as a new parent. The company offers a unique course, promoting knowledge and normalisation to prevent mental health issues in the early years of parenting. The business was a finalist as New Business Start Up 2021.

Stacey is also a Daisy First Aid franchisee, having trained 10,000 parents in paediatric first aid. In addition to saving lives with her training, she has been highly commended as Most Inspiring Business Parent of the Year and Against All Odds. Stacey won Franchisee of the Year in 2019 at the Family Networks Awards.

https://linktr.ee/staceycann

www.parentinginmind.com

# CHAPTER 18:

## Theresa Nye

---

### If the rug is pulled, what then?

If your only source of income was suddenly stopped, what would you do? Do you have a plan B?

### Plan A by default

I had never really been one for planning in my personal life and certainly had no ultimate career plan. In almost 40 years of working, I have only had four jobs, the last of which lasted 29 years! I joined the company, a newly established events agency, when I was 28, in 1992. The time was right for a new challenge. A friend introduced me to the business owner who was looking for some support in his new business but didn't know what he needed, and she assured me, "I am sure you are it!"

I was indeed 'it'. A great career blossomed. I was able to travel the world as an Account Manager and later Director, organising conferences and managing trade exhibition booths from the design concept through to on-site delivery. I would often be away on back-to-back events and, being single, it suited me. Of course, I missed out on many a social event and family time with the result it was pretty much impossible to plan, as the travel took priority. Life was good and I didn't think too much to the future, other than taking out a pension plan. I was in a secure job and happy to coast along.

Twenty years into the role, business was booming and I was settled. Too settled. I hadn't realised but I had fallen into a clinical depression, I was still delivering but had lost my spark and was running on auto pilot. I was lucky in that my boss recognised that something wasn't quite right and urged me to seek medical advice. I did, but only to stop him nagging at me as I felt OK but hadn't realised I was in a rut of what had become normal. I duly got my diagnosis and prescribed medication.

I recovered, vowed to recognise the signs in future and act accordingly. Thankfully, any dips in my mental health since then have been minor. The business continued to grow and thrive, but I knew long term I didn't want to travel as much.

I volunteered to take on the role which I had identified as becoming more and more important: being the point of contact for our biggest client in terms of procurement and all that goes with being on the preferred vendor list of a major pharmaceutical company.

I was happy with this new mix in my workload until I started to feel the need for more free time some eight years later, in 2019. I had seen a new business model gaining traction – the five-day working week being done in four days. I thought it could work for me and I raised it as a point of discussion. However, as we entered 2020 with a full order book of conferences and exhibitions, the time wasn't right to take this further. I put it on the back burner and then boom! The rug was pulled from me, a course of events I couldn't control had started.

The first reports of Covid-19 were coming through and our clients were starting to talk about postponing their events. Those postponements soon became cancellations and suddenly my long career in the live events industry was slipping away, and it wasn't on my terms! The UK Government's job retention scheme was launched and I found myself 'furloughed'. I had the extra time I had been craving but no idea what to do with it, my options were limited in any case as we were now in a pandemic. I took diploma courses in Life Coaching and Social Media Management. After a few weeks it was clear that this situation was not going to be a short-term blip, it was looking bleak, and with live events relying on mass gatherings, some serious discussions were needed with my employer.

As many staff as possible were kept on furlough, but some were made redundant as there was no way of knowing when things would return to normal. I knew I had to get my plan B in place, but with most of my experience being in trade exhibitions I had to dig deep.

## Saying goodbye to Plan A

I looked at myself, my skills and experience, and becoming a freelance Project Manager in exhibitions was not an option for obvious reasons, so I decided I would investigate being a Virtual Assistant (VA).

## Finding Plan B and beyond

I set up my business, Treehouse Project Management, to offer my services on a project basis. I created a website, social media accounts and started networking on Facebook. Early on in this part of my journey I decided being a VA wasn't for me. Although I was organised and had a lot of experience in an office environment, I wasn't disposed to the typical VA tasks. That said, I managed to get a couple of small jobs via social media and this was a great confidence boost.

The months went on, summer came and went, and the UK was bracing itself for a second wave of Covid-19. The events industry was on its knees but companies including the one I was still furloughed from had moved into virtual events, but these were not at the scale of what we were used to pre-pandemic, so the projects were only open to a small team. I continued to work on Treehouse Project Management, building my online presence and doing what was needed to establish it as a bone fide business including opening a business bank account and getting the name trademarked. I found in the VA discussion forums there were a lot of people who didn't know where to start in setting up their business; to me it was intuitive, and I found myself helping people and essentially giving away my knowledge for free. A business coach gave me some good advice, which I took and set up a group with a view to producing a course on how to set up a VA business and offering one-to-one coaching sessions.

I was now coming up with so many business ideas and felt excited at what was possible, but at the same time I was scared. My earnings had plummeted, and furlough was not going to go on forever, so I had to make this work. My problem was, I didn't know anyone I could approach as a potential client, I didn't know anyone in business as my friends were teachers, nurses or worked in events. To remedy this, I joined a business networking organisation which met online with the premise of the membership referring business to each other.

At each weekly meeting you can promote your business, and although I had joined in the VA category, I drew on my procurement experience and promoted myself as someone who could help small businesses grow and obtain larger contracts through bidding and tenders. Within a few weeks I had my first enquiry from one of the members who had the opportunity to bid for a large contract (£150,000). I guided them through the paperwork, produced the proposal document, and when the company was shortlisted, I attended the online presentation as an extension to the company. The presentation went well, and they won the business. What a boost!

It was at this time I entered Treehouse Project Management into the Centre of Excellence awards, and in February 2021 was announced as the winner of the Entrepreneur category. What a great start to the year, my social media went crazy when I posted about this success.

My second piece of business from my network group came from a landscape company who wanted to bid for a contract worth £93,000 to make over a school garden; once again my client was successful. 2021 was going from strength to strength.

The furlough scheme came to an end and Treehouse is thriving. Who knew I had it in me! I certainly didn't, but from not thinking I had a plan all those years ago, I sort of did! It just wasn't formulated but I had gained the experience and business contacts, which is serving me well now. Additionally, I now have contacts in different industries, and with transferrable skills I have something to build on.

I am currently working with a medical communications agency who I had previously worked in partnership with when I was full time in events; we stayed in touch, and I now have a contract with them to manage the production of a series of webinars.

The biggest lesson I have learned in the last two years is not to rely on one source of income. I have all the tools needed going forward – resilience, experience, contacts, flexibility, resourcefulness, a positive attitude, and the ability to apply myself and work hard – and have now joined the dots and don't intend to stop at Plan B!

## Theresa Nye

Theresa Nye was born in London in 1963 and grew up with three younger brothers with parents who had a 24-year age gap, her father being 51 when she was born. From the age of seven she spent school holidays in Kent with the elder sisters of her father, where she developed an interest in all things vintage.

After 25+ years in the events industry, she is now the owner of Treehouse Project Management, working with small businesses in their business development programmes by supporting with bids through a procurement process as well as managing virtual and live events.

In her first six months in business, Theresa won an award, 'Entrepreneur of the Year', and continues to build on this success while finally getting her work-life balance in order, with the renovation of her home in Kent, where she stayed as a child, as an ongoing project.

www.treehouseprojectmanagement.com

www.facebook.com/treehouseprojectmanagement

# CHAPTER 19:

## Tracey Smolinski

---

**Changing your mindset for success and to build long-lasting relationships**

In decision theory and general systems theory, a mindset is a set of assumptions, methods, or notations held by one or more people or groups of people. A mindset can also be seen as arising out of a person's world view or philosophy of life.

Mindset is a way of life and it changes from person to person. Some people are negative and some are positive, but mindset can have a massive impact on your life whichever way you turn. People who know me know that I have a very positive mindset and I believe that is the key to success in your business and your life. The glass is half full, not half empty, so to speak.

Mindset is a simple idea discovered by world-renowned Stanford University psychologist Carol Dweck in decades of research on achievement and success – a simple idea that makes all the difference. In a fixed mindset people believe their basic qualities, like their intelligence or talent, are simply fixed traits.

"In one world, effort is a bad thing. It, like failure, means you're not smart or talented. If you were, you wouldn't need effort. In the other world, effort is what makes you smart or talented."
– Carol Dweck

A **fixed mindset** is the belief that intelligence (or any ability) is a *fixed* trait that you're born with and can't do much to change. People with a fixed mindset spend their time documenting their intelligence or talent instead of developing them. They also believe that talent alone creates success – without effort.

A **growth mindset** is the belief that their mind can be developed and grown, which then opens their minds for learning and growing through the power of a positive mindset, thus giving them the tools and belief for success. In other words, people with a growth mindset think their mind can be developed for their growth.

I believe in a growth mindset. What's the point in being negative? Negativity breeds negativity, whereas positivity breeds positivity. I know what I would rather be and always think of positivity all the way – surround yourself only with those that are positive, BOOM!

A growth mindset, as Dweck calls it, is pretty much exactly what it sounds like: a tendency to believe that you can grow. In her book *Mindset: The New Psychology of Success* she explains that while a fixed mindset assumes that our character, intelligence and creative ability are static givens which we can't change in any meaningful way, a growth mindset thrives on challenge and sees failure "not as evidence of unintelligence but as a heartening springboard for growth and for stretching our existing abilities."

I truly believe that those people that have the right positive mindset will flourish more than those that don't and that anything is possible if you believe in yourself and your ability. You just have to plan, prepare, initiate and **take action** to reach your goals and dreams, otherwise guess what? Nothing happens.

This is important because it can actually change what you strive for and what you see as success. By changing the definition, significance and impact of failure, you change the deepest meaning of effort. By having a growth mindset, by reframing things, you can really alter the mind for the better. Let me give you an example.

Rather than saying something like 'I would love to be able to buy a house', say to yourself, 'What do I need to do to buy a house? How much do I need to save or earn? How long will I need to put money by or what can I do to add more income to my pot in order to achieve my dreams?'

By having a fixed mindset and saying 'I cannot afford to buy the house', straight away you put up a block or a wall, giving you the mindset that you cannot afford it. By thinking negatively, negative things will happen or you will stand still. Have you ever heard the saying by Napoleon Hill, *Whatever the mind can conceive and believe, the mind can achieve?* So if you think and believe you can achieve, you will. If you think you are a failure, well then you are. Changing to a growth mindset can literally change your destiny.

How many times do you hear of super successful entrepreneurs that have said their teachers have told them when they were in school that they would never make anything of themselves and how many times these entrepreneurs have proved them wrong? There is a lot to be said for teachers that have said that.

## Why does growth mindset matter?

Being aware of a growth mindset is also important for recognising businesses and employers who value this in their working environments. When companies embrace growth mindset, their employees report feeling far more empowered and committed. They also receive greater organisational support for collaboration and innovation, making the workforce more motivated, eager to succeed, which creates a more engaged environment for company growth.

If you want to achieve your potential in order to build long-lasting relationships, or to have your workforce achieve their potential, or have your students or colleagues achieve their potential, growth mindset is a necessity. It should be part of your DNA. Imagine if everyone went around with negative thoughts, there would be complete negativity in the world. Scary thought, I always like to look at the positives and say, 'Well yes this is a problem, however let us look at the plus or good things.' I am a great believer in the Law of Attraction, you attract what you think. Look back and think how many times do you say to yourself, 'Oh, I am having a bad day today.' Guess what happens: bad things, things go wrong or negative outcomes happen. By thinking positively your day will be a lot more positive. Try it out, it really does work. We all have good and bad days but it is how we deal with things that makes the difference.

To surround yourself with positive and successful people is the best way forward. They only want to be around other positive people. Funny how we see that millionaires and billionaires usually hang around with other millionaires and billionaires because they are of the same mindset; positive and successful thought leaders stick together.

So let me give you some examples in your working environment and personal life.

You go on holiday to a Caribbean island expecting sunshine every day. It rains every day, so you have two choices. You either moan about it, sulk and stay indoors or just moan all day, *or* you say, 'OK so what can we do today? Let's explore!' You then go somewhere where perhaps you may not have gone had it not rained *but* it turned out to be the most beautiful place and you were so pleased that you visited. You take the most fabulous photos that you will cherish forever. Priceless. Creating memories seeing beautiful places is awesome. That is what life is all about – spending time, seeing and creating experiences with loved ones. Nobody can take happy memories away from you. So can you see what happens when you embrace a positive mindset and attitude? Good things happen. Now try doing that all the time. See where it takes you.

So how do you change into having a positive growth mindset rather than a negative fixed one?

- Be self-aware, know what your strengths and weaknesses are

- Develop a strategy to hone in on your talents

- Don't fear failure and turn failure into learning, the bigger the failure, the bigger the learn

- Cultivate a sense of purpose

- Be confident which builds self-esteem

- View challenges as opportunities

- Try different learning strategies

- Stop seeking approval and just own what you decide to do

- Celebrate your wins with others and celebrate their wins

- Reward actions not complacency

- Take criticism as constructive

- Disassociate improvement from failure
- Reflect on your learnings regularly
- Place effort before talent
- Learn from other people's mistakes
- Be humble and abandon the image and ego
- Use the word 'yet' (e.g. 'not mastered it *yet*')
- Make a new goal after the goal is accomplished
- Cultivate grit and determination
- Never give up
- Take risks in front of others showing authenticity
- Be realistic about time and effort
- Take ownership over your attitude
- Emphasise growth over speed
- Be open to change and opportunities

When you implement these strategies it will take you to another stratosphere and then the magic starts to happen.

So go out there and connect, learn and grow with that positive mindset for success in your business and life.

# Tracey Smolinski

Tracey Smolinski is a serial entrepreneur, property investor, founder of award-winning global business network Introbiz, author of *Master Networking* and creator of networking tool Fortune in the Follow Up. She is also a motivational speaker, mentor and networking coach. She loves people and genuinely loves helping and developing others. Tracey has raised over £200k for charity and loves to make a massive difference for the good.

Tracey is passionate about helping people network effectively and wants to teach and develop entrepreneurs and business owners to become successful networkers, to create a winning referral economy for their exponential growth. Her goal is to impact and connect a million in five years which has a massive positive impact on the economy.

In her spare time, you can usually find her walking on the beach with her three Cavachons, Coco, Barney and Boo, and chilling with her partner, children, parents and friends.

info@introbiz.co.uk

www.introbiz.co.uk

www.iwowglobal.com